SACRED SEDUCTION

BY KITTY CAVALIER

A GUIDEBOOK, MEMOIR AND TRIBUTE
TO THE ART OF SEDUCTION

TABLE OF CONTENTS

For Eve

ACKNOWLEDGEMENTS

Thank you to my family: Mom, Dad and Sib, for always encouraging me to be myself no matter how much my job titles may have made you blush.

Thank you to Qoya and its founder Rochelle Schieck for teaching me how to live an embodied life, and that superpowers do exist under our very own skin when we stop to feel them.

Thank you Veronica Varlow for pioneering the world of seeing seduction from a different perspective, and for being my gypsy muse.

Thank you Betsy Prioleau for your incandescent writing and relentless perseverance to tell the true story of seduction. You inspire me beyond words.

Thank you Jo "Boobs" Weldon for teaching me burlesque, which was the catalyst to feeling seduction in my body.

Thank you Regena Thomashauer a.k.a Mama Gena for initiating me into the world of the divine feminine, teaching me the discipline of pleasure and for showing me that my desires are not too big for me.

Thank you Barbara Stanny for your immense support and your sacred teachings, without which this book and the very concept of sacred seduction would not exist.

Thank you Nikki Garrett, Sandi Firecracker, Kelly Garone, Dana Lawrence and Mindy Goldstein for being my first repeat clients. Your ongoing hunger for my work is what has kept the embers stoked and growing. I am so grateful.

Thank you Andrew Blahnik for believing in me so deeply for so long, and for inspiring my seduction journey in so many ways. I am forever grateful for you.

Thank you Emily Burns for all the girl talk, and for being one of my great muses.

Thank you Beth Mayesh for being my supportress and fellow sorceress, helping me divine the message of sacred seduction in so many, many, many ways.

Thank you Vivi La Voix for teaching me what it means to live a life that is surrendered to the sensual and for being my sister in seduction.

Thank you Carol Bloom.

Thank you Kevin.

Thank you Shauna Haider for designing this beautiful book and for taking the seed of my teachings, waving your wand of creativity and making magical things.

To all my students, blog readers and finally, to you who are reading this book — thank you!

Seduction is a way of life.

INTRODUCTION

Seduction.

Say it.

Out loud.

Let the soft "s" slide over your tongue. Let the blunt "d" press against you. Allow the sharpness of the "c" to make you blush, and the "tion" to finish everything perfectly, like a fine glass of port after a gorgeous meal.

Seduction is something that may intrigue you, confuse you, anger you or delight you.

Most likely, it does all that and more.

Seduction is a power we have been taught to both fear, and secretly revere.

We are told that it is a manipulative, cunning, sexual way of getting everything you want no matter what the consequences. That it is a way of convincing or swaying others to do things they don't want to do, often by using their own vulnerabilities against them. Seduction is presented as being dangerously sexy. A kind of irresistibility that can wreck a home or destroy a life.

What I am here on this page and on this Earth to tell you, is that there is a lot more to the story of seduction than what you have been told.

Love, sex and romance is just one square on the Rubik's Cube of seduction.

I believe that when we are in love with and approving of ourselves, and unimprisoned by our insecurities, seduction is something that happens naturally.

When we feel confident in our bodies and are able to flaunt our flaws with pride, we are undeniably magnetic. When we are not needy or dependent on another person's approval to define our worth, we give off an air of irresistibility.

Don't get me wrong, it's not that I don't fawn over the side of seduction that is all lingerie and lipstick, but to me, these things are extensions and expressions of our seductive power, not the source of it. Seduction is so much more than just a game played between lovers.

Because it has been under the thumb of a smear campaign for the last several thousand years, collectively we are only able to access it from one dimension. But to look at only this side of seduction is like looking at a rainbow and only seeing red.

Seduction is like a diamond: at first what looks like a hundred prisms explode into a million when we are willing to let in the light.

In this book we will be looking at seduction from all different angles, illuminating elements that have been blotted out over time. I will take you on a journey to understanding the true nature of seduction: a way of connecting to and carrying out our power and our purpose on this planet, and practicing the law of attraction with your body, mind and soul.

We will be covering the more traditional elements — how to tease, how to entice, how to leave others wanting. But when we are able to realize the full scope of what sacred seduction has to offer, these skills become its side effects not its source.

True seduction is magnetism, not manipulation. It is the power to attract. It is a practice in surrender, and a practice in restraint. It is a dance of savoring, being in the present moment and feeling EVERYTHING.

Seduction takes guts. Seduction takes smarts. Seduction requires trusting the voices inside of you, rather than the voices outside of you. Seduction is the new law of attraction. Seduction is a spiritual practice.

Seduction is a way of life.

HOW TO GET THE MOST OUT OF THIS BOOK

Play With Me in the Parlor

As a sacred seductress, you are the one with all the answers. Not me, not this book. This book is designed to take you on a journey into your own inner labyrinth to create the unique code of captivation that only you possess.

In this book there are exercises called Parlor Games that accompany each topic. These games are designed to inform and enhance your understanding of each element of sacred seduction.

I highly recommend that you do these exercises in the moment, even if that means just scribbling something down on a cocktail napkin and tossing it in your purse.

Seduction lives in the moment. Often we wait until we have acquired the perfect journal or until we have had time to think things through, and then they never happen. I urge you to take immediate action!

Use those answers that first pop into your mind. They are the most electric; they contain the most potent charge. Get on that lightning bolt and take a ride, baby!

Feel free to play the parlor games multiple times. Our inner seductress is always changing and evolving. You may find your answer today to be different than the one you had yesterday and different from the one you have tomorrow. Embrace that side of you that is a shape shifter.

Climb Every Mountain, But Not All At Once

It is important to remember that in the practice of exploring and expanding our relationship to the sensual, every woman is way different. Some of the exercises in this book may seem easy as banana cream pie, and some of them may seem as insurmountable as Kilimanjaro.

Expanding your seductive power is a revolutionary act, no matter how big or small. What you will learn about sacred seduction is that there is really no way to do it wrong. Just simply by picking up this book you have already done everything right.

Create Your Own Seduction Society

"Genius Loves Company."

— *Ray Charles' final studio album*

One of the most important and effective pieces of creating seductive success is having a community of women to support you. Reclaiming seduction as a sacred practice is no small feat my friends. Ask any revolutionary: allies are not optional.

This is why I highly recommend creating your own Seduction Society, a group of women with whom you can practice and play with what you are learning. You can do this by creating weekly gatherings, an e-mail group, a Facebook group or any chain of communication that allows you to share your journey and be each other's cheer squad in the process. Share everything with society members; do not hold back. Play the parlor games together.

Reveal whatever changes you are noticing as a result of reading this book, no matter how small, and cheer your seduction sister on like your life depends on it.

Seduction takes a village; we do not act alone. Bridging the gap between women and eliminating the stench of competition around seduction is one of the most liberating, world-changing things you can possibly do. Not to mention, you get to have a ball with your babes.

What's not to love?

"Never complain,
never explain."

— *Katharine Hepburn*

CHAPTER 1

REDEFINING
SEDUCTION

In 117 Words Or Less

I believe that seduction is a sacred practice. I believe in the intoxicating beauty of authenticity. I believe in things that sparkle both on the inner and the outer. I see seduction as a feminist art. I believe that Eve was not only innocent, but that she was a genius for picking that apple. I trust in how things feel over how they look. I think red lipstick makes everything better. I live as though life itself is my lover. I seek to protect and cherish the secrets of sacred seduction. I live in service to seeing you give the world what it is longing for: the reclamation of your seductive power, and the use of it to cast your spell.

The Full Story

Let's start, as all great stories do, with something embarrassing. When I was a kid, I used to make out with everything. I practiced kissing on my hand, the wall, the poles of my swing set, dolls; you name it. When I would play house it was not just a play kitchen I would use to set the scene. I would spread out a picnic blanket on the front lawn, put on my best dress, and bring all sorts of mundane snacks from the kitchen that would magically transform into luscious delights. Ritz Crackers became chocolate-covered strawberries and grape juice stood in for the finest champagne. I would pretend I was sitting there, basking in the sun, cradled in the arms of a great love.

It wasn't so much love or having a boyfriend that appealed to me.

It was living with sparkle, merriment and magic. Romance was not some gesture of frivolity. It was the JUICE. One year, for my parents' anniversary, I baked a cake, set up a candlelit meal (TV dinners that I microwaved) and played host for the evening, providing them with an unforgettable night of refinement and romance.

The home I grew up in was deeply religious. I went to Catholic school all the way through 12th grade. Growing up, the world didn't seem like a safe place for my magic to thrive and my passions to unfurl. Over time, this magic began to fade. I thought I had thrown it away or lost it, but really what I did is pack it up and lock it in a special place in my heart to be brought out into the light when the world was good and ready.

As I entered puberty, I felt a desperate need to fit in, but never could get the round curves of my soul to suit the square angles that were being asked of me. I coped with this by developing tremendous insecurity, an eating disorder and a nasty, bitter hatred for my body. For years I abused my body with compulsive bingeing, starving and bulimic behaviors. Everything revolved around what I ate or didn't eat. If I was being "good" around food and exercise, I was flooded with a high of absolution for my sins of not being enough. However, these baptismal waters were easily muddied by anything "bad". Even an innocent Hershey's Kiss could blow me out of the water, back to where I thought I belonged. My body was my battleground. The place where all my grief, disappointment, shame, fear, and anxiety was held. And if she would just cooperate, I could have it all.

At age 21, I moved to New York City. Slowly, the dust on that special box in my heart started to move. In this environment that was so different from my little town of a thousand people, uniqueness was celebrated rather than hidden. All of a sudden those sharp angles of the box I was trying so hard to fit into started to expand and soften. Coloring outside the lines was more than okay; it was the new requirement to fitting in! I was happy in my new home and new life, but also scared shitless. I now felt like a small fish in a big ocean, and my attempts to control this fear through food and weight were worse than ever. I thought that until I could achieve the perfect body, there was no way I could be loveable. After so many years of struggling so hard, I was almost on the verge of giving up.

Living in NYC has its perks, one of which is access to a burlesque show every night of the week. (If you are unfamiliar with burlesque, it is a type of performance art that is characterized by a striptease.) I found the thought of stripping extremely threatening, but also liberating. What I saw at the first performance I attended changed my life.

There onstage were women who looked just like me, but they were not covering up their "flaws". They were flaunting them with a raw sex appeal that was irresistible. Even more surprising, was that they ranged in age from 23 to 50-plus. Size A boobs to size G. They had real bodies, the kind of bodies you'd see in the locker room at the gym. The kind of bodies I feared more than death — NORMAL ones! What struck me the most about them is that they made the rules. The look in their eyes and the sparkle of their energy easily communicated that there are no such thing as flaws here.

The audience was completely spellbound by their sparkle, their beauty and their glow. They were not waiting for anything on the outside to change or become "perfect" to experience their own raw beauty, power and sensuality. I was hooked. I was in love. I was changed. And I left there thinking, "Wow, if they can feel that way without having to achieve perfection, maybe it's possible for me, too."

I now had a new mission in life. Rather than seeking to feel confident through achieving perfection in form, I sought to find the perfection in exactly who I was. I threw myself into learning everything I could about this kind of feminine empowerment. I read books, took classes in burlesque and sensuality. I joined pole-dancing classes, women's studies groups; anything I could get my hands on. I not only absorbed the information, I put it into action in my life no matter how scary or how uncomfortable it felt. One of these bold actions was to perform my own burlesque striptease in front of 250 people.

Even though I would rather have flown to Spain and run with the bulls than take off my clothes in front of strangers, I mustered all the courage I had and went for it. I seduced the crowd as I stripped down to pasties and a G-String. I stood there. Literally naked. Totally vulnerable.

To my surprise, instead of being my worst nightmare, it was my greatest triumph. All those things I told myself I would have to change in order to be lovable; all the times I had tried to abuse my body into submission; all the times I denied myself pleasure because I thought discipline and restraint was what it took to win in life — all of it melted away as I stood there and received my applause. I streamed tears of joy and relief. I felt beautiful and powerful. I loved myself, inside and out. And I didn't have to change a single thing.

I did not know it at the time, but what I was physically acting out was the archetype of the journey of the sacred seductress. Our culture portrays the seductress as being a conniving femme fatale temptress hell-bent on eating her prey for lunch like a black widow spider. Either that or she is a vapid, sex-crazed tootsie here solely to service the sexual fantasies of others, namely men.

Oh people, it is time for a paradigm shift.

The type of seduction I teach is not a game of control, manipulation or ego. The type of seduction I teach — what I call sacred seduction — is an exercise in surrender. Sacred seduction is attraction through authenticity. It is taking the mask off rather than painting one on. Sacred seduction is something that lives inside of us. It is a power we all possess.

Sometimes we think that in order to look or feel more seductive we have to dress a certain way, speak a certain way or act a certain way. These things can be catalysts to our inner seductress but they are mere expressions of that which already exists within us, our unique seductive code.

The seductress is the ultimate empowered woman. She is a woman who accentuates her flaws just as much as her assets. She sees the beauty in everything. She has a keen connection to her intuition and trusts herself more than anyone or anything else in life. She uses her erotic power to light up the world. She is embodied, sensual and free. She is captivating and compelling. She loves every ounce of herself and thinks that she is just the bee's knees. She lives in deep service to seeing her divine soul weave the magic that only she can create in this lifetime. She is a bold risk taker, a force to be reckoned with, and a cheeky, sassy dame.

My mission in life, my greatest passion, is guiding each woman to remember her inherent seductive nature, and create a world where her inner seductress cannot only come alive, but where she can thrive. Simply by reading this page, I know you are starting to feel the tides of seduction as a spiritual practice swell within you. Come on in. The water is warm. Don't worry if you don't know how to swim. That's why I am here.

I will teach you.

RE-DEFINING SEDUCTION

Traditional Definition of Seduction:

1. To lead away from duty, accepted principles, or proper conduct.

2. To induce to engage in sex.

"Yes, please."

— *Veronica Varlow*

One of the first questions I usually ask someone who is wishing to learn more about the art of seduction is: "What have you been taught about seduction?" Of course, the most common answer is: "Nothing." As children and young adults, many of us are taught to avoid the topic of seduction like the plague — that it is a sinful, evil practice that is reserved for those on a wayward path. Or if we are taught to embrace it, something about this style of influence doesn't quite feel right. Perhaps you saw an Aunt using her cleavage and eyelashes to get out of a speeding ticket. Did it embarrass you, delight you, make you angry? Or perhaps you had a Dad whose charisma made him a little too well-liked by his female co-workers. Did you ever try your own hand at seduction only to be shamed and laughed at, leading you to reject it ever since? Or are you the type who has so much seductive power that it scares you? You enjoy being able to attract attention sometimes but are not exactly sure how to receive it. Or you don't enjoy the attention you attract so you dim your light to keep away the moths.

Wherever you are, wherever you've been, I honor you and I welcome you. Please, pull up a velvet cushion. I am so thrilled that you are here. Whatever you have been taught about seduction I am going to ask you to pack up in a train case and leave outside the door for now. You can always pick it back up when you leave. But let's clear the slate, draw a fresh canvas, and allow me to take you on a tour of seduction as I have come to know it.

First, I invite you into a secret room, a room with a door that looks like part of the wall and opens onto a gorgeous salon of beauty with hundreds of fresh flowers, plush couches, a beautiful altar and tapered candlelight. I lead you to a dressing room, where you take off whatever you are wearing and slip into a soft garment that is so beautiful and comfortable that it makes you feel like you are both naked and wearing a fabulous outfit all at the same time. Or, if that garment is not really your style, I open the door to a glorious closet filled with gorgeous wonders of beauty and glamour. I instruct you to choose the item that feels best for you right now. A sarong? A vintage cocktail dress? A bright Indian sari? A vinyl poodle skirt and spiky bra? A satin robe, a pair of cashmere pajamas, a man's tailored shirt? This is your time, your style. Find what seduces you the most in that dressing room and don't look back.

Next I invite you to curl up in a pile of pillows. A seduction handmaiden enters and she immerses your feet into a gilded bowl of warm lavender-scented water filled with rose petals. She then takes a mixture of fine salt and frankincense oil and massages every inch of your feet and legs, encouraging you to sink deeper into the pillows you are lounging on, and just receive. Once your feet are blessed and soft as a flower petal, she surrounds them with a warm towel that is so plush it feels like a hug.

Then, you curl up with me on the couch amongst curls of incense. The aroma hypnotizes you into even deeper relaxation. I then regale you with tales of great seductresses, stories of courage, romance, glamour, sizzle and spark. Once you have been fully inspired and intrigued, I ask you to tell me some of your own. I praise you for your triumphs and reframe your foibles to be acts of utter brilliance. You begin to see that seductive power is not something you need to go in search of, it is something that has been a part of you all along.

And this is just in the first twenty minutes.

Oh, the places we'll go!

When you imagine yourself in this scenario, how do you feel? Relaxed? Beautiful? Pleasured? Permissed? In sacred seduction, our attractiveness is expressed not in how we look, but in how we feel. The measure of our seductive success is not just the consequence we have on others, it is the depth of deliciousness we can feel when relishing in being exactly who we are. In this state, magic can happen. Our enjoyment becomes a centrifugal force that draws exactly what we want towards us at warp speed, everything from the trivial to the tremendous. The ability to seduce lives within all of us.

"I don't seduce, I surrender."

—*Albert Camus*

GOOD GIRL/ BAD GIRL

Make a list with two columns titled Good and Bad

ANSWER THESE QUESTIONS:

1. What were you taught about seduction?

2. How do you feel about seduction today?

3. How do you feel about the idea of being a seductress?

THE LEGEND OF SCHEHERAZADE

When we imagine the icons of seduction according to the current paradigm, the classic cast of glamazons comes to mind: Ms. Monroe, Ms. Jolie, Ms. Kardashian. But let us now pause and open our minds to a story of truly sacred seduction: the Legend of Scheherazade.

Once there was a Sultan, who after being betrayed by his wife, had taken to marrying a new virgin bride every day. The morning after his wedding he would order the new bride beheaded out of anger at the transgressions of his first wife. He was convinced his bride's early death was the only way to keep her faithful. Until he encountered Scheherazade.

Scheherazade, the daughter of a political advisor, spent most of her time reading hundreds of books. She ravenously consumed information on everything from poetry to philosophy, science, art, history, war; anything she could get her hands on. After passionately pursuing her own education, she became a magnificent storyteller with a wit as sly as a fox.

Against her father's wishes, Scheherazade volunteered to spend one night with the Sultan. Once in his chambers, she asked if she might bid farewell to her sister. When her sister entered the room, Scheherazade began to tell her one last bedtime story. The Sultan listened with awe.

As dawn broke, Scheherazade stopped in the middle of the story. The Sultan asked her to finish, but since the day had already arrived, there was not time. He decided to spare her life for one more day to finish the story the next night. So the next night, Scheherazade finished the story, and then began a second, even more exciting tale, which she again stopped halfway through, at dawn.

So the Sultan again spared her life for one day to finish the second story. And so Scheherazade kept herself alive day by day, leaving the Sultan eagerly anticipating the finishing of the previous night's story.

At the end of one thousand and one nights, Scheherazade told the Sultan that she had no more tales to tell him. But of course, he had already fallen in love with her, and over time she had borne him three sons. Having been made a wiser and kinder man by Scheherazade and her tales, he spared her life, and made her his Queen.

PARLOR GAME

GOOD ᴀɴᴅ BAD

What is different in this story of seduction compared to what you have been taught about seduction?

WHO IS THE SACRED SEDUCTRESS?

OLD PARADIGM	SACRED SEDUCTRESS
Femme Fatale — brings death and ruin through her manipulating her erotic power	Femme Vitale — brings life, joy and inspiration to everyone she meets through surrendering to her erotic power
Her sexuality is used as a commodity	Her sexuality and sensuality is hers alone, and is used to light up the world
Gets what she wants, often through force or manipulation	Attracts what she wants through magnetism and surrender
If she does not succeed in seducing, her power is diminished	Is always open to a greater plan
Is always the one in control, is always the seducer	If she does not succeed in a seduction campaign, she trusts that rejection is just a form of protection, or that there is more fun to be had in the attainment of what she wants
Leaves others wanting by never being vulnerable or showing too much of herself	Loves to be seduced and trusts the tides of her desire as being a direct line of communication to the divine
Mean and bitchy	Leaves others wanting by maintaining her boundaries and leading a life that is so full of things she loves, she doesn't depend on others for her fun
Maintains a cool, flawless exterior therefore she can never be hurt	Understands that her vulnerability is the most attractive thing about her
Lives from a place of ego, control and pride	Fierce about her boundaries
	Embraces her flaws and sees them as some of her greatest assets, living them out loud with pride and enthusiasm
	Is grounded, real and true
	She gives up her ego and her need for control in service to loving bigger and feeling more

SEDUCTRESS

Seduisant

Seductora (Spanish)

Séductrice (French)

czarodziejka (Polish)

Seduttrice (Italian)

Vamp

Vixen

Femme Fatale

Bombshell

Fox

Siren

Temptress

Flirt

Coquette

Tease

Provocateur

STORIES FROM THE
SEDUCTION
COUNCIL

*I asked some of my most seasoned seductresses
what it means to be a sacred seductress.
This is what they had to say:*

"Seduction is something I do for my own delight in the moment. It has to do with sensual preparation — intentionally creating an environment that draws sensuality and pleasure out of me. It has less to do with influencing others and more to do with creating my own pleasure."

— Nikki, 39
Educator, artist and musician

"Before finding Sacred Seduction it was all about SEX. Now it's about living my life in a pleasure filled way. It's become about paying more attention to what seduces me, not about how I can seduce the guy, the other person, but instead what am I desiring and how I can be more seduced by those things in my life."

— Sofia a.k.a. Gabby Garnet a.k.a. GG, 51
Awesome Homeschooling Mom and Sacred Seductress

"Growing up I thought seduction was dirty, manipulative; it was a tit for tat type of thing. Taking classes with Kitty turned my definition upside down. I was able to reframe my life through the eyes of the sacred seductress and how I had the power within me to call in what I needed and what I wanted. My life is certainly much more fun because of it."

— *Laura, 32*
Lifestyle, Career Coach, Expert Shimmy-er

"I used to think seduction only applied to romance and wooing. Now I see how it applies to every aspect of life, even things that most people would never associate with seduction — like illness and motherhood."

— *Sandi, 33*
Mother, artist, songstress, and glitter fiend

"Seduction is intuition allowed to bloom and sparkle...this is what Kitty has taught me. It is all of the senses, including the sixth, in charge of one's decisions, feelings, and actions, allowing the heart to lead and the mind to follow. It is decidedly feminine, extremely powerful, very vulnerable, and completely intoxicating to experience. Under Kitty's tutelage, I have realized how important, empowering and definitive it is to allow oneself to be immersed in the sacredness of the act of seduction."

— *Eliza, 42*
Mother, stepmother-to-be, conjurer, lingerie enthusiast

CHAPTER 2

SENSUALITY AS A SUPERPOWER

WHEN I AM CONNECTED
TO MY SENSUALITY:

- I say what I want when I want it.

- I eat to fullness without needing to eat more than what feels good.

- I have incredible sex.

- I have an easier time doing the things I often resist, like exercise and file papers.

- I can handle conflict, disagreements and discomfort with grace.

- I feel unstoppable.

- I am able to listen to and be present with others.

- I take bigger risks.

- I trust that everything is going to be better than okay.

- I put more faith in the present and how things are than I do in the future and how I wish things would be.

- I slooooooowwwww down.

- I taste, touch, hear, see and sense more deeply.

- I know before I know.

- I tell the truth more often.

- I fucking love being alive.

Sensuality.

Feels like looking at still, glassy water.
Or stirring thick chocolate brownie batter.
Or like feeling the flush that blushes your
cheeks when a new lover takes your hand.

---

sensuality

Definition: relating to or consisting
of the gratification of the senses,
or the indulgence of appetite.

Sensuality can be a loaded term. Often it is associated solely with the workings of sex, but when we distill sensuality to its true essence, its true nature, sensuality is quite simple. It is no more and no less than experiencing life through our senses.

Exploring our sensuality does more than just bring out more flavor in a strawberry. Sensuality requires us to slow down and feel. A sacred seductress is keenly connected to her ability to feel. She trusts instinct over impulse. Being able to trust the sensations of the body allows us to trust more deeply the stirrings of our heart.

Have you ever been faced with a tough decision and after some deep relaxation, all of a sudden you just know what to do? This is why meditation is so helpful, because it quiets the squalls of anxiety in the mind, allowing us to connect to the still waters of truth. When we slow down and feel, our mind becomes our counsel and ally, rather than an authoritative judge.

The deeper meaning here is that when we are attuned to the senses we are deeply aligned with the divine itself. Goddess, God, The Universe, The Freaky-Honey-In-The Sky — whatever you want to call it — expresses itself and communicates with us through sensual pleasure. The crunch of a frozen raspberry against our teeth on a sweltering day, the smell of rosemary being carried on the wind from an herb garden on the windowsill, the rapture of seeing the ocean crest over a hill while you ride your bike down a dirt road; experiencing these simple pleasures through our sensual body makes that elusive mysterious VIP club called heaven truly a place on Earth.

Exploring the sensual does not have to be extravagant. The simplest pleasures are the finest. When you can take pleasure and nourishment from something as basic as the caress of a cotton ball as you remove your makeup after a long day, the world becomes your oyster, your sensuality the pearl.

Being able to feel deeply and with total abandon is at the heart of practicing sacred seduction. It fosters our connection with intuition — the jet stream that keeps sacred seduction in motion. "Trust your gut, go with your instinct" — these phrases exist for a reason. Have you ever interviewed at a job that has all the trappings of being your dream career, but something just doesn't feel right? If you ignore that inner voice (as I often have), you may find out three months down the line that the company is actually corrupt. Or the person who had the resume of a champion that you expected to be your mentor turns completely inept and inadequate, and you are actually the one running the show behind the scenes. Or maybe you randomly decide to take the scenic route home one night for no explicable reason, and all of a sudden you find yourself driving behind the car of your best friend. You pull over and by crazy coincidence find out that she or he decided to take the scenic route for no reason also, which results in a glorious evening walk together along a fragrant cedar trail littered with the petals of pink flowering trees.

That voice that tells you to do something irrational, or even downright crazy, is often the wisest sage you will ever encounter. The voice within that tells you when something feels right — that voice *is* right.

Whether your connection to that voice is loud and proud or that setting has been on mute for your whole life, follow me seductress, and we will make that inner voice your new best friend. Within the remainder of this chapter you will find exercises, games, ideas and adventures that invite your sensual animal to come out and play. These are perfect parlor games to play with your Seduction Society. You can do one of them or all of them. However many you choose to do, even if it is none, simply by reading these words you are investing in your sensuality. For that, I honor you.

Knowing yourself sensually makes you an unstoppable woman. Every joy, triumph, longing and answer you have ever searched for exists right there underneath your own skin.

Wonder Woman, eat your heart out.

- Play a piece of beautiful music.

- Close your eyes and feel your way through your home with your hands. Pay attention to the feeling of every texture available to you, and see if you can experience your home in a way you never have before through the sensations under your fingertips.

- Turn on a song with a great bassline and dance to the entire thing as if you are the drumbeat come to life.

- Walk through nature and smell everything. The grass, the dirt, the trees, the rocks. Then, on a different day with different weather, go through and smell everything again, noticing all the subtleties in aroma.

- Create a touch salon with a few different objects that have unique textures. Lay them out on your bed and use them to touch different parts of your body, feeling every sensation available.

- Take deep breaths and use your breath to massage your ribs, lungs, spine and belly as you breathe in and out.

- Visit a spice market. Indulge in aroma!

- Watch a beautiful movie.

- Gaze at the clouds and give yourself a mystical reading with the shapes you see, like a fortune teller reading tea leaves.

- Cut images out of a magazine that inspire you and paste them into a scrapbook. Then, look back at all the images and see if you can piece together some of the common threads in your visual tastes.

- Go on a walk and take a camera. Take photos of things that you would not normally notice or photograph.

- Go to a flower stand and gaze at all the beautiful flowers. See if by simply gazing at the flowers you can start to smell their aroma.

- Go to a museum and let your eyes play!

- Slowly turn a bottle of glitter in the sunlight.

- Scrub your entire body with a body scrub made of sugar or salt. Feel every inch as the giver and the receiver simultaneously. Don't wait for an event for which you want soft skin to do this. This is just for you.

- Before bed, wash your feet in the tub slowly and deliberately. Massage the soles of the feet with pure lavender essential oil. Then slip under the covers.

- Light a stick of incense and use the curls of smoke to write your wishes in the air.

- Keep an energizing bottle of essential oil like eucalyptus or citrus on your night stand. First thing in the morning, place a few drops on your palms and inhale three times.

- Turn on some music and roll around on the floor, using the earth as your massage therapist!

- Choose a designated part of the body (like the lower legs) and grab some lotion or oil. Set a timer for five minutes and massage just that part for the full five minutes, seeing how much you can feel, and if you can locate some hidden parts to your body you didn't even know existed.

- Apply oil to your legs and feet. Without using your hands at all, let your feet and legs lovingly massage each other to bliss.

- Heat a vegetable based oil on the stovetop or in the microwave in a pretty container until just warm. Pour it into a gorgeous bowl or tea cup. Step into the shower and slowly, sensually pour the warm oil all over your gorgeous body. Massage the oil into your skin, and when you feel complete, do a quick rinse. Even after the rinse you should still have the silky softness of oil lingering on your skin.

- Write love notes to yourself and hide them in boxes and drawers, inside compacts and under pillows. Surprise yourself with beauty and love!

- Organize one tiny part of your home, like your sock drawer or a shelf in your medicine cabinet. Throw out what you don't love and make what you do clean, organized and pretty. The sensual loves atmosphere!

- Hold eye contact with a stranger for a second longer than you should through a bus or train window. You may never see that person again, but for this moment, your connection is all that matters.

- The next time you take a sip of water, wine or your morning coffee, follow the entire journey rather than just savoring the sip. Bring your sensual presence to every moment, from when you pick up the glass to the moment you put it back down.

L'AROMATIQUE: THE ART OF SEDUCTIVE FRAGRANCE

When I was 15, every Friday night I would go cruising at the mall with my girlfriends. We would always stop in a certain bath and body store to douse ourselves in fruity body splash. When no one was looking, I would wander into the back of the store where they displayed the more expensive stuff and load up. When I say load up, what I mean is that I would pull a piece of index card out of my wallet and spray it with a cologne called Woodland. It was the fragrance worn by my crush, with whom I was hopelessly in love, but felt far too afraid to ever make a move on. It was much easier to just keep him in my wallet. Oh if that boy could see me now!

Let's explore a powerful and magical art: the art of seductive fragrance. First, a little science lesson in why fragrance plays such a central role in sensuality and seduction. When we inhale a fragrance, it enters a bulb of nerves in the nose called the olfactory system. This system is deeply connected to the limbic system, the part of the brain and psyche that governs our memory and emotion. Hence, by keeping that little card in my wallet, pulling it out and taking a deep breath, I could make my heart swell and my loins tingle any time I wanted them to!

In the book, *La Seduction: How the French Play the Game of Life*, Elaine Sciolino writes: "A sophisticated and alluring perfume can play a central role in a seduction campaign. Drawn to the scent one is drawn to the person. Lured by sensation that cannot be expressed in words one is tempted to suspend rational thought and follow the lead of emotion."

But seductive fragrance is more than simply drenching ourselves in gardenia and expecting the world to come running. In fact, overdoing it can have quite the opposite effect. In the book Sciolino interviews Jean-Claude Ellena, a master French perfumer. He says: "The American vision of perfume is what I call performance. Known for long duration tenacity and power. Some perfumes immediately create distance because their smell is so strong that I go like this." (He extended his arm as if to push her away.) Perfume functions almost like a shield."

What Ellena is insinuating is that perfume's role in seduction is to draw someone closer, not drive them away. Applying your seductive fragrance is about a lot more than finding your pulse points.

A seductress perfumes her body in a way that is ritualistic, adding her special magic to use her scent to cast a spell. As Coco Chanel said when asked where to apply perfume: "Wherever one wishes to be kissed."

Enjoy this Seductive Fragrance Anointing Ritual, which will connect the power of your fragrance to the power of your intention. I love, LOVE my perfumes, but for this ritual I prefer to use essential oils. Essential oils are like the blood of plants. They are extremely powerful and aromatherapeutic. One of the reasons I love to wear them as fragrance is because their potency is inviting and hypnotic, rather than forceful. Because they originate from natural sources you run a much lower risk of offending or off-putting when applying in the quantity required for this ritual.

After performing this ritual you will walk down the street and turn heads in every direction. Everyone you encounter will want to come closer to you and be struck with confusion as to why they cannot stand to be away from you.

It's our special secret, seductress.
And I'm not telling a soul.

ESSENTIAL OIL

ANOINTING RITUAL

Take a few drops of your essential oil and apply it to each area of the body outlined in the ritual as you say the incantation out loud or in your mind. Feel free to use different essential oils throughout the ritual or just one. If you are sensitive to fragrance or just in a pinch, coconut oil, body lotion, or hell, even just plain water will do! Remember, it is not the object but the intention behind it that will actualize your soulcraft.

1. Root Chakra
Base of spine and above pubic bone

May I feel my rootedness today. May I feel my roots reaching deep into the core of the Earth. May I remember that there is no separation between me and the hot magma center of the Earth, and that I am supported by this connection always.

2. Sacral Chakra
Pelvis and lower belly

May I be filled with the energy of sensual creativity today. May the bowl of my pelvis be filled to the very top with pleasure and radiance. Let the slow sway of my hips set the pace for every thought I think, every word I speak and every action I take.

3. Solar Plexus
Upper belly

May I live this day from my gut. May I trust above all how things feel inside, regardless of what they look like on the outside. Let me trust my gut completely today.

4. Heart Chakra
Chest and heart

May the sacred garden of my heart blossom wildly today. May any blocks or barriers from the raw, untamed growth of my heart dissolve, and may I live with a wide open, shining, loving heart.

5. Throat Chakra

May I cast spells with my words today. Let my words be shaped by the sensual vibration of these energy centers in my body, and may I make this world a better place by fearlessly living and speaking my deep truth.

6. Third Eye Chakra
Between the eyebrows

May I open to the infinite wisdom that lives within me, and trust that I always know the answer.

7. Crown Chakra
Top of the head

May I be filled with the magic of stardust today, the light of the heavens, and a roaring stream of divine love and energy. May I bring this love and feminine power into every single thing I do.

A MENU FOR
T̲H̲E̲ SENSES

One thing I am really good at is creating romance on the fly. Early in my career as a seductress I would be frustrated by anything that would present a challenge to my sensual adventures, particularly the cold, dark New York winters. This was until I learned how to work with the challenges of creating romance rather than against them. Cold and dark weather outside meant a greater opportunity to create a warm, candlelit, sensual atmosphere inside. Enter the art of the L.R.P. — the Living Room Picnic.

The living room picnic is something you can do alone, with a lover, or with a group of friends. Spring, summer, winter or fall, LRPs are easy, delicious, and often a catalyst to even greater adventures on the picnic blanket. (If those living room walls could talk.)

Remember: Seduction is not just the culmination of a desire, it is the enjoyment of everything that desire has to offer from its conception to its completion. Seduce yourself as you prepare for the LRP. Wear a sexy apron, listen to music. Clear your workspace so that you have a clean, uncluttered slate to start on when preparing your courses. Always use the fine china.

Take a bath or shower and wear something that feels perfect for lounging around on the picnic blanket. I like to wear a vintage slip with a dressing gown that falls easily off my shoulders. Wear jewelry. Adorn yourself. Smell good. Feel good.

THE LIVING ROOM PICNIC

1. Set a gorgeous blanket on the floor and sprinkle it with rose petals.

2. Light tons of candles (like, way more than what is necessary).

3. Play music that seduces and hypnotizes.

4. Set out sumptuous treats filled with simple aphrodisiacs (recipes to follow).

5. Eat everything with your hands.

6. Take your sweet, sweet time and luxuriate in your indoor paradise for as long as you like.

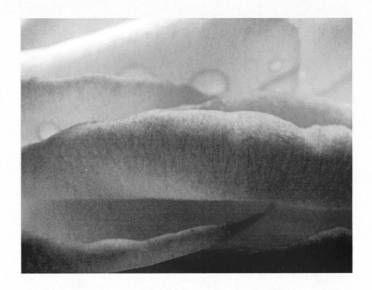

Furnish your experience with delicious delights. These are some of my favorite, easy-peasy recipes for LRP. I give you full permission to leave the dishes until the morning.

Olives

Olives are a perfect food to be eaten with the hands, or a toothpick. This allows for lots of tease and play while you rest the plump, oval fruit between your teeth and slowly draw the toothpick away. Many grocery stores have antipasto bars, so choose a variety. Olives look gorgeous when arranged on small, individual plates and shimmer like the Mediterranean itself against the glow of candlelight.

Figs with Ricotta AND Honey

Take one look at a fig and you will know that Mother Nature is quite the little vixen. At the market, choose figs that feel soft to the touch (but not squishy). When you've brought them home, take a moment to inspect the gorgeous purple color on the outside of the fig, as well as its curvaceous shape — like a juicy set of hips.

Cut the figs in half and observe the flesh inside. It is the definition of succulence.

Once the figs have been cut, arrange them on a beautiful plate in a way that pleases you.

Take the ricotta cheese and spoon a small amount on top of each fig.

Then, take golden honey and slowly drizzle over the figs, dousing them with sweet nectar. I like to use just a little too much honey, which necessitates finger licking later on.

Roasted Asparagus

Wash asparagus and trim the thick ends. (You can save them and freeze them to make home-made stock for seductive soups down the line. Yumma-yumma.)

Steam asparagus in a saucepan until it has softened outside and its color has deepened, but it should still be crisp in the center.

Drain the asparagus and pour about a tablespoon of olive oil in a skillet.

Once the olive oil is heated and shimmering, add the asparagus. A little moisture left over from the steam is good; it will help with the cooking.

Sear until its skin is just browned.

Place the asparagus on a gorgeous plate and season with sea salt and fresh ground pepper.

Squeeze some lemon juice and grate some lemon zest on top.

Eat slowly and suggestively with your bare hands.

Mini Sangria

One of my favorite things to do in the summer is buy very ripe, dripping peaches, cut them into slices, and stack them at the bottom of a wide wine glass.

Pour a lovely wine (red or white both work) atop the peaches until they are almost covered. After your wine is gone, the fun has just begun as you can now delve into your little wine-soaked slices of heaven.

Chocolate Sauce

Buy a bar of your favorite kind of chocolate. Over very low heat, add a splash of milk to a small saucepan. Follow that with a few chunks of chocolate and stir with a wooden spoon.

When that chocolate has melted, add a few more pieces and a bit more milk until you get a nice, warm, gooey ganache.

Serve in a beautiful bowl with a side of fresh, hand-whipped cream.

Accompany your dippable delights with pieces of fruit, torn croissant, cubes of pound cake and fresh mint leaves.

CHAPTER 3

CONSCIOUS ATTRACTION

Attention, like seduction, is something we both run to and run from. Attention can feel so good, so validating. It lets us know we are important, attractive and alive. But it can also come with tripwires. We may feel guilty or undeserving, or incapable of handling it. Shining our light also puts us at risk for a type of attention we don't like, so rather than run that risk we just choose not to shine at all.

Living as a sacred seductress means living in full expression of one's power, beauty, strength and individuality. Like moths to a flame, this attracts attention. A seductress is a woman that is confident in her powers of attraction.

This chapter is going to teach you how to enhance your powers of attraction and feel comfortable, deserving and right on about any measure of attention that comes your way.

Magnetism

allure   *drawing power*   *magic*

attraction   *pull*   *spell*

fascination   *charm*   *charisma*

appeal   *enchantment*

draw   *seductiveness*

THE QUEEN'S WALK

Let's do an experiment.

Walk from one side of the room to the other. Just normal. Just walk.

Now, I want you to do the same exact thing but this time, let your feet lead the way. As if your feet were your brain and your body were just following along.

Now, let your head lead the way. (We call this one "The New Yorker".) Imagine you are so immersed in your own thoughts that you forget you even have a body.

Now, this time, you are going to do the same walk, but you are going to lead with your hips. As if your hips were the conductor and your body the orchestra. This is not about trying to look sexy or trying to move your hips in a certain way. Just let your hips take the lead.

Did leading with the hips feel any different?

Finally, continuing to allow the hips to lead, press your heart forward. Imagine you have everything the world is hungering for right there in your heart, chest and breasts. Pretend you have world peace in your breasts, sister. Let's serve it up. This is not for the benefit of others; it is simply to honor and celebrate the miraculous gift of your feminine body, and allow the benefits of that pleasure to ripple out and heal the world. Hips and heart. Surrender to that. See how that feels.

What did you notice?

Congratulations! You just did your very first Queen's Walk. The first of many, I hope.

When walking the Queen's Walk, we walk slowly with not the destination in mind, but all the pleasure that awaits us as we make our way. Our essence precedes us and enters the room long before our physical body appears. We walk with elegant and relaxed posture, shining our light forward for all to see rather than slouching and trying to hide.

We move like we are making love. Most importantly, we walk slooooooowly. From the moment our foot touches the earth, we are enraptured. Our lips cannot help but curl into a secretive smile, and our eyes are unafraid to roam and make contact with whomever and whatever they wish -- knowing that those fortunate enough to meet our gaze have been blessed. Most of all, we take our time.

A Queen is never in a rush.
She is always right on time.
Her time.

THE

QUEEN'S WALK

Practice the Queen's Walk for the distance of about one block per day.

Notice with simple curiosity the effect that harnessing the power of your movement has on the world.

Share the results with your Seduction Society. Gradually increase the frequency with which you practice until you can call on the Queen's Walk anytime, anywhere.

"*I didn't discover curves.
I only uncovered them.*"

— *Mae West*

SEDUCTION COUNCIL

THE QUEEN'S WALK

"When I do the queen's walk I feel I am patiently and confidently drawing all my wishes toward me, rather than trying to plow into them."

— *Nikki*

"When I am doing it, really doing it — heads turn. Really, no lie. So I experiment with it, I'll do it for a block or two, then I purposely stop for a block or two and every single time — heads turn, comments are made, but only when being the Queen and walking her walk!!! Love this exercise . . ."

— *Sofia a.k.a. GG*

"After my very first class with Kitty, I had people telling me I carried myself differently. It was the walk. Even if I am not doing it fully, when I am mindful of how I am walking, people notice. Once when I was out with a few girlfriends, I was gushing about the course I took, and the Queen's Walk. They asked me to demonstrate, right there at the restaurant. I obliged and walked myself right smack into one of the waiters. I said "Oh I am so sorry!""

He smiled and said "No, thank you!" ;)"

— Sandi

"Every woman loves learning how to be a Queen!! The Queen's Walk is a way to remind myself on a daily basis of my inner siren and her desire to be a free spirit as opposed to a woman stuffed in a suit!"

— Grace, 40
Freethinking woman; encourager; healer; dancer; mother and graceful lady

"The Queen's Walk is I guess a form of walking meditation. It reminds me to come back to my power center when I'm feeling off. Everything slows down and I am able to become present in that moment."

— Coco Divine
Angel rock star, sacred sedActress & priestess of love

As the expression goes: "It's not what you say, it's how you say it." In my former life as a corporate trainer, I would have the task of seducing anywhere from 5 to 500 people at a time. It didn't matter how compelling the information was that I was delivering. If my confidence, my pace and my energy were not set to the dial of seduction, the result would be like instant Ambien.

When you see a seductress in action, she is often the mysterious woman at the center of the party that has a crowd leaning in while she holds court. Use these tried and true seductive speech practices to cast your spell. As my friend and teacher Veronica Varlow likes to say, "Words are your wands."

Turn the page

When reading a book there is that moment, however brief, where we turn the page. Our minds and hearts get a momentary respite from the consumption of information. During that time we integrate all that we have read up until that point. So it is with our spoken words. To add an instant seductive quality to your speech, pause for just two beats between sentences the next time you are telling a story. Practice this with a girlfriend. For extra credit, at the height of the story, pause for a full five seconds as you hold eye contact to build the anticipation.

Less is more

Often when we are speaking, we feel the need to tell all. That we must get our point across, otherwise it feels like a string has been left untied. Play with keeping a little of the story for yourself. Like leaving a bite of chocolate cake uneaten on the plate, leaving a bit that is unspoken leaves others wanting more.

Speak the change you wish to be

What you say becomes your reality. Our words act as magic

wands to carry out our destiny. If you say you are insecure, meek and un-seductive, then that is what you are. If you say you are hot, gorgeous and the most seductive thing to hit planet Earth in the last 5,000 years, then that is what you are. Words have power. Handle with care.

Indulge the element of surprise

Betwixt. Clandestine. Cockalorum. Lubricious. Do you find your ears perking up at these unfamiliar sounds? Seduction is all about intrigue. Peppering your sentences with words that have a mysterious quality will draw others closer to you as it shows that you speak your own secret language, and that you know how to make what is old and unknown brand new again.

Galvanize with the honest and unexpected

Conversations full of fluff that is just meant to impress another are a SNOOZE. When you say what is true, rather than what you think you should say, the air fills with electricity. Like a splash of cool water in a dark, stuffy room, the truth wakes us up. It galvanizes both the speaker and the listener alike. Be willing to wake up the world with your truth. Not only does the world need your truth, it begs for it.

STATING THE TRUTH

Most people are familiar with the use of mantras, phrases that are thought or spoken over and over with the intention of reinforcing or creating a positive belief. Mantras are powerful blocks for building the container of your seductive power. The term, mantra, however rings to me of a thought on lease. Rather than a thought that you repeat to yourself in the hopes that it will become your reality, why not just state the truth?

The following statements are simple truths about every woman that walks this planet, if she chooses to admit them.

- I am so hot, it's ridiculous.

- My curves heal the world.

- My eyes, my lips, my thighs, my breasts, I just can't decide which I like the best!

- I am divinely beautiful.

- I have never looked more gorgeous than I look right now.

- I am a mesmerizing, sensual creature.

- Everything about me is gorgeous.

- The world longs for me to say yes to my seductive nature.

- My beauty is mine. It never fades, and it can never be taken away.

- There is world peace in every delicious inch of my body.

- Beauty is my divine birthright.

- I honor the divine when I honor myself. I am Goddess in the flesh.

STATING ᴛʜᴇ TRUTH

Think of your own "stating the truth" and share with your Seduction Society.

Extra credit: Write one of these feminine truths in second person tense. (i.e. you're so hot it's ridiculous.) Write it on a sticky note and place it on a public bathroom mirror for the next anonymous seductress to delight in!

"Darling the legs aren't so beautiful,
I just know what to do with them."

— *Marlene Dietrich*

Seduction means something different to everyone. Who are your icons of sacred seduction?

PARLOR GAME

INSPIRATION

Make a list, a Pinterest board or a collage of people you find seductive.

Notice what traits they embody that you wish to enhance in yourself. Imagine that your list/collage is like a big box of clothes to play dress up with and go wild!

What is it that you love about them? What are their styles like? Their energy? What makes them seductive to you? This is not so that you can be like someone else, it is to identify how these seductive traits resonate and enhance the ones you already possess.

MY OWN JOURNEY OF BRINGING CONSCIOUSNESS TO MY POWERS OF ATTRACTION

When I walk down the street lookin' foxy, it used to be that my main intention was to be noticed by men. Male attention simultaneously delighted and disgusted me. I wanted to be able to enjoy the pleasure of dressing to feel sexy just for myself, but was frustrated by the inner collision of feeling both validated and violated at the same time. Seductive power felt like a lightsaber I couldn't control. At times it would surge unexpectedly leaving me burned. Other times it would flicker on and off, leaving me weak and defenseless.

Finally one day I decided, enough of this shit.

What flipped the switch to me being able to enjoy my femininity, my beauty, my seductive nature and my sensuality for me? I began to approach my seductive power and the attention it drew with curiosity rather than a need for validation and control.

What I found was a softening of my judgements and a firming up of my energetic skin. I grew to feel compassion towards myself and others, and a new level of enjoyment when my radiance received recognition.

Remember, a seductress is a woman who is confident in her powers of attraction. Does the candle resent the moth? Does the flower shame the bee? Hardly. They embrace their intoxicating ability to attract, as well as the consequences of that attraction, with elegance, regality and pure uninhibited surrender.

There is a big difference between attraction through narcissism and attraction through sheer magnetism. The difference, again, is consciousness. Being conscious of our intention allows us to steer the ship of our own allure. The success of a sacred seductress is not measured by how much she gets, it is all about how good she feels.

"Receive everything, decide later."

– *Rachel Owen*

Grazie! Danke! Merci! Dalu! Natick!

A simple thank you is neutral ground. It is gracious, but not gratuitous. No qualification or negating the compliment with something that muddles its potency necessary. Just say thank you. That's all you need.

Enjoy it!

Your presence on this planet is prolific. As Marianne Williamson says, "Our deepest fear is not that we are inadequate. Our deepest fear is that we are powerful beyond measure. It is our light, not our darkness that most frightens us."

Take one for the team; we all win!

Over to Marianne Williamson once again: "As we let our own light shine, we unconsciously give other people permission to do the same. As we are liberated from our own fear, our presence automatically liberates others."

Act as if …

Like most things with seduction, if you don't know how to do it, just act as if you do. Someone tells you that you have a gorgeous smile. You don't really know how to take that in. Well, imagine someone who does. How would they react? Do that. Fake it 'til you make it, sister. Works every time.

Take it in

Sometimes when we receive a compliment there is an impulse to boomerang it back to that person and compliment them. If that feels true for you in the moment, great. But this can also be a tool of deflection. Hold it right there, sister. This isn't tit for tat. Deflection leads to depletion, for the giver and the receiver alike. Take it in. Your willingness to receive is actually the gift in itself.

DEALING WITH UNWANTED ATTENTION

When unwanted or unsavory attention comes your way, first of all, if there is ever a situation where you feel unsafe, get out of there. There is a big difference between attention and harassment. You have a responsibility to yourself to be discerning with the attention that you choose to accept and encourage. If something doesn't feel good, walk away.

The way I deal with unwanted attention is to firmly assert that I do not wish to engage with that person. If the attention persists, I leave the scene, or I calmly tell them the truth by saying, "This is making me uncomfortable" or "Please, stop". Being annoyed vibrates on the same frequency as unsavory attention itself. Telling the truth deflects the energy, and shows that not only will you not be passing the ball back, you're not picking it up in the first place.

Does my sexiness upset you?
Does it come as a surprise
That I dance like I've got diamonds
At the meeting of my thighs?

— *Maya Angelou*

CHAPTER 4

SEDUCTION: THE SCIENCE AND THE ART

> *"Beauty and seduction, I believe,*
> *is nature's tool for survival,*
> *because we will protect what*
> *we fall in love with."*
>
> — *Louis Schwartzberg*

Okay. Time to get down to business. We've done a lot of focusing on the why. Now my pets, it's time to shift on over to the how. (Rubs hands together with a devilish smile!)

I would like to dedicate this chapter to my Mother.

My Mom has been one of the greatest teachers of seduction in my life. Maybe not in the way you might imagine (i.e. taking me shopping for corsets instead of training bras or teaching me how to tell the difference between a Bordeaux and a Pinot noir.) My Mom has been a great seduction teacher because she is a very tough nut to

crack. Learning how to overcome her resistances by working with them rather than against them has been one of my crowning seduction achievements.

When I was a kid, I had a pretty easy time manipulating Mom into my own guilty pleasures: splurging on McDonald's for dinner and taking me shopping for clothes way too often. I knew how to beg, how to dangle carrots of things I knew she wanted, and how to craft a story that wasn't quite a lie, but wasn't quite the truth either. This was an excellent learning experience of what manipulative seduction looked and felt like. It felt gross.

When I look back on those days, I get an icky, bad feeling when I think of how I was a classic, cranky, unsatisfiable teenager who would do anything to get my way.

As an adult, when I want something from her or for her, it is because I want to enrich her life. Sometimes these things are attractive to her, sometimes not. She is no easier to seduce now that I have matured; in fact it has become even harder. In this chapter I will be sharing some core theories of how to seduce, illustrated by stories of me and my Mama Bear.

1. Make the experience an easy, irresistible delight

"You catch more flies with honey."

I remember one time asking my Mom to come with me on a retreat in New England. She hates to travel so I knew that no matter how dazzled or desirous she felt about the retreat itself, the travel piece was a dragon I would have to slay.

So, I made sure that every stop along the way was a garden of delight. I asked my Dad to dress in a suit and act as her chauffeur on the long drive to the airport. He created a trail of rose petals from the house to the car and packed her a gourmet picnic lunch. I made her a playlist of awesome music and sent it with a packing list of everything she'd need for the weekend so she wouldn't have to think about a thing. I told her I couldn't be there to pick her up from the airport, but I would hire her a private car. Of course, when she stepped off the plane and into baggage claim, there I was with a huge sign decorated with a thousand stickers and her name in big block glitter letters.

By taking all these steps, I made the thing she was dreading the most into one of the most rewarding parts of the whole experience. When I look back on the weekend, the retreat was wonderful, but the seduction itself? That is something that neither I nor my Mom will ever forget.

2. Enthusiasm can move mountains when it comes from true desire, rather than need

One day I got a call from my Mother and heard her voice, very excited on the other end of the phone. "Guess what I just did!?" she asked. "What?" I replied. "I seduced Uncle Freddie!" she said.

Any other daughter might be a bit unnerved by this news, but I knew exactly what she meant.

My Mom lives in a small South Carolina town and her brother, my Uncle Fred, lives in Florida. For years, she had been wanting Fred to come visit her and my dad, stay in their home, and see their new life in retirement. But because the drive was a very long car trip and there were no airports close by, it never seemed to work out. One day, when she was on the phone with my uncle, she stated once again her desire to have him come to visit.

Because she is my star student and has taken every one of my classes, she knew that trying to convince him (or even worse, guilt him) was not going to feel good for either of them, nor would it get her what she wanted. So, with all her bubbly enthusiasm, she communicated how much it would delight her to have him visit.

Unattached to the outcome, she relayed how much fun they would have, and how deeply she wanted to spend time together, showing off her new hometown. The enthusiasm in her voice was like a hot air balloon sailing into the sky that he couldn't help but want to hitch a ride on. He said yes, and arrived at her doorstep two weeks later.

There is nothing more attractive than being wanted and not needed.

The key here is that she unabashedly communicated her desire without any attachment to the outcome. The stench of expectation and obligation would have weighed down that hot air balloon like a bag of rocks, giving her desire no hope for lift off.

By keeping with the delight of simply desiring a visit from Uncle Fred and being open to any adventure that might present itself, she made her request irresistible. Go Mom.

3. Unattainability fuels desire

Betsy Prioleau, the author of *Seductress: Women Who Ravished the World and Their Lost Art of Love* explains that "The great goddess was not easy of access. Pilgrims reached her shrine through a long, dark, circuitous, labyrinthine passage, a sacred journey commemorated in the meander and spiral designs on their relics. With the labyrinth as the paradigm of seduction, seductresses made themselves difficult. They led men a dance, provoking, teasing, thwarting, and disappearing around the next bend. Programmed to this arduous archaic Seductive Way, humanity puts no value in erotic prizes easily won. Love philosophers belabor the point: 'What's granted is not wanted'; 'Dearness gives value to the meat'."

Once I had a lover who pined for private photos of me. It wasn't a naked photo he wanted. I have many racy photos on the Internet — not fully nude, but showing a lot of skin. What he wanted were photos that no one else had ever seen. He wanted to be privy to a private show of images that reflected my private life and inner world. So, one Thursday, I initiated the following exchange:

me: hey you. i know you've been asking for a photo that is taken for your eyes only. it's thursday which is my lucky day, and it might just be yours too.

him: really?

me: yes. if you are willing to pay the price that such a treasure exacts.

him: which is?

me: first, you must send me a line from your favorite piece of erotic poetry.

him: lol, i don't even know what that means. plus i'm at work.

me: well, then we shall have to wait. but you know…there is this thing called google and you can access it from the very phone you are texting me on right now

him: alright let me see what I can find. what do I search for?

me: erotic + poetry. the only requirement…is that it must dazzle me.

him: ha! ok, here I go.

Two hours later after an exhaustive search, my suitor completed his task with flying colors. A photo of my creamy thigh and hip ornamented by a vintage garter belt and French lace stocking was his reward. Actually, I sent him a bounty of three photos that day to honor his efforts. Do you see how if I just randomly sent him the photo how much less of an effect that would have had?

In setting up this little scavenger hunt, I demonstrated that an image from my private arsenal is something of extreme value, making it more satisfying for him to receive and for me to send. Also, by creating a task for him to do I opened his mind to an experience of the erotic that he previously did not even know existed.

When we go to a restaurant that charges $25 for a cheeseburger and serves it on a porcelain plate as big as the table itself, for some reason it tastes better. When we get invited to a party, other obligations may get in the way or we may feel too fatigued to make it out. But if the party is secret, a VIP invitation that is only happening once with no plans to repeat, we are much more likely to show up. Have you ever had the scales of your purchase decision tip to "yes" when you see that there is only one of that garment left in your color and size?

Unattainability is not about withholding, it is about creating and standing for our value. When we value what and who we are without compromise, the world responds accordingly.

THE ART OF SEDUCTIVE RESTRAINT

"If it's not a hell yes, it's a no."

A great seductress knows the power of restraint. She worships at the shrine of wanting. Living in a constant state of arousal requires us to leave certain things unsatisfied, for wanting cannot exist when there is nothing left to desire. This requires us to learn the art of leaving others wanting, but even more importantly, the pleasure of leaving ourselves wanting.

This is often the most challenging part of being a Sacred Seductress. In our culture we are taught to say "yes" to everything. Take on as much as we can and please everyone no matter what. How many of us have ever put up with something that is un-pleasurable, or even downright painful, just so we could avoid the discomfort of saying "no"? Most often the reason we find saying no to be so uncomfortable is because we are afraid of meeting another person's disapproval.

Well ladies, get ready for me to blow your mind.

Your ability to say no is the key to being liked, adored and admired.

Let's say that again: Your ability to say no is the key to being liked, adored and admired.

A real seductress knows what she wants. She knows when she wants it. She also knows what she doesn't want, and she is unafraid in expressing all of this. A woman who owns her No is a pleasure to be around, because you never have to worry about her doing something solely to please you. She is never a bore, because she never says yes to something that bores her. A woman who owns her No is a woman who can teach you a thing or two, you can sense it. She is someone you naturally want to be around because you know you can trust her. You know you can trust her because you can tell she trusts herself.

Saying no is a practice. Experiment with saying no to others, as well as yourself. Leave a bite of chocolate cake on the plate. Don't send that text to your newly ex-lover. Turn down that party everyone is going to that you simply don't want to go to. Say no to that extra project at work. What you will undoubtedly notice is that your life, career and relationships will begin to flourish, rather than crumble.

Restraint is not loss. It is the opening, the creation of space for the things we really want the most.

PARLOR GAME

PLAY WITH THE TENSION OF WANTING

These may sound like torture, but the object here is to enjoy the pleasure of unrequited desire.

You can indulge in these desires anytime you like, but for right now, see what it feels like to just enjoy the sensation of wanting, knowing that you do not need that object to feel a sense of gratification.

- Go into your favorite store without your wallet.

- When you receive a text or an e-mail, look at that person's name for a moment before you open it, enjoying the anticipation of what they may have to say.

- Leave one sip of wine or one bite of food unsatisfied.

- Go into a bakery and look at all the glorious treats, enjoying the salivation.

- Spend a night with a lover where all you do is kiss, or even less.

- When you are listening to someone, nod less. Just take time to take it all in.

- Tell a story slowly, with fewer words than usual. If you don't get every detail, don't worry. It's good to keep a few secrets to yourself.

SEDUCTION: A FORMULA AND A FORCE

Seduction is a great many things. Predictable is not one of them. There are elements we can control and elements we cannot.

How seduction happens is this:

$$attraction + action = seduction$$

1. Attraction

Attraction is something chemical. It is a force of sheer magnetism. It is when vibrational forces align and come together. It is something we have very little control over, but what control we do have is governed by our:

2. Action

Action is physical steps we take to inspire desire. Think of action as being like the sails on a ship and attraction being like the wind that moves it along. There is, however, one crucial missing element to this formula: Who is steering the ship?

In a later chapter we will go more in depth into how to refine your efforts of allure through the art of seductive surrender. For now, let's take a look at some of the building blocks of this formula of attraction.

What's the guaranteed way to ensure seductive success? Let's ask the experts.

Imagine you are in a cafe and you notice someone who catches your interest. All of a sudden, three epic seductresses — Frida Kahlo, Josephine Baker and Mae West appear before you as your seduction counsel. When asked what to do, Frida says: "Go over there, order a double shot of tequila for both of you and ask them if they have ever contemplated their own death, and if so, how they would do it."

Noted.

Josephine says "No, no, no darling! You must force the band to play 'The Birth Of Swing' and start gyrating your body like a snake in the grass."

Okay.

Finally, Ms. West saunters into the spotlight of your attention, demanding that you go over there and fan yourself. When this gathers the person's attention say, "Oh sorry sweetheart, are you suddenly feeling hot in those clothes? Don't worry. It's just me."

With so many different opinions, what's a girl to do?

All three of these approaches are excellent and historically proven to get you what you want.

But remember, as a sacred seductress, rather than relying on how we think things should look, we trust deeply in how things feel. What approach feels right to you? Tequila, gyration, provocation, or something completely different?

Authenticity is at the heart of what makes a sacred seductress different from the traditional perception of seduction. A sacred seductress is deeply connected to her instincts and she follows them without hesitation, despite what external influences might say. She is not afraid to receive counsel, but it is her inner authority that always gets the last word.

*"As soon as you trust yourself,
you will know how to live."*

— *Johann Wolfgang von Goethe*

HOW TO FEEL MORE SEDUCTIVE

Whenever I do a Q and A with my students one of the most common questions to come up is: "Kitty, how can I feel more seductive every day?"

The answer is different from what you might expect. Seamed stockings and French perfume need not apply on this one.

The answer is actually a question in return: "Well, if you want to feel more seductive, first tell me, what is seducing you my darling?"

Usually when women ask me how to feel more seductive what they are really asking is how they can feel more sexy. Well, what makes you feel sexy? Is it a long hot yoga class followed by a long hot bath and a long hot lovemaking session? Is it taking a day off just to read a gorgeous novel cover to cover? Is it fresh flowers in every corner of your office in a vibrant, sexy color? A new outfit? A new lipgloss? A new pair of Dr. Martens?

To feel seductive we must align ourselves with the sensations of that which we want to feel.

In contrast, let's say you have a big meeting coming up at work and you want to seduce your team into greatness and your clients into putty in your hands. How to feel more seductive in the boardroom is a different game altogether. When you envision how you want to feel in this seduction, what is the word that comes to mind? Most likely it is a feeling of power.

So, what makes you feel powerful? A well-rehearsed pitch? Bangin' shoes? A delicious breakfast that makes you feel amazing? A mantra? The game may be different, but the rules remain the same.

PARLOR GAME

FILL IN
THE BLANK

WHAT MAKES ME FEEL _____ IS:

1. Sexy. 2. Powerful.
3. Relaxed. 4. Alive

There you go. Now you have a complete menu of how to feel more seductive in each area, written by your very own hand. All you have to do is surrender!

Imagine with me: It's Friday night. You pass a chocolaterie in town and wish to bring your lover home a surprise of her or his favorite dessert.

Upon arriving home, you enter the house with a box from the bakery and place it in the refrigerator, forbidding your dearest from opening it. All night, every time your lover opens the fridge she or he feels the electricity of surprise and desire.

You then instruct your lover to take a long bath or shower and when she or he enters the bedroom, the box is waiting there on the bed wrapped in a thick black ribbon.

You give your significant other the satisfaction of slowly untying the ribbon, feeling the satin slide against itself as the bow falls open like a blossom.

Then, you take the ribbon and playfully tie it in a blindfold around your lover's eyes, further heightening the intensity of the tease. You open the box, taking your time. You retrieve just a bit of the dessert onto your fingertip and caress your lover's lip.

At this point, your partner's entire body is straining with yearning to solve the mystery of what is inside that box. Finally, you place the first bite of dessert on your own tongue, and present your lover with the long awaited answer to this delicious riddle by means of a deliriously passionate kiss.

Now isn't that better than getting home and yelling out "I brought dessert" as you hang up your coat in the closet?

Teasing and being teased is one of the most outrageously fun sandboxes of seduction one can enter.

Here are some ideas and games designed to inspire you in the art of artistic anticipation:

- Secretly deliver one stroke to your lover in the most inappropriate of places on his or her body, while in the most inappropriate places in public, such as a crowded train or while in the kitchen alone at a family gathering.

- When sitting at dinner with friends, send your lover a racy text or photo, even though you are sitting right next to him or her.

- When your lover arrives home and you are not there, leave a scavenger hunt of clues that lead to things like your panties, a bottle of oil for massage, champagne in the refrigerator, having the hunt end in a gorgeous photo of you in the buff, holding up a sign that says "Welcome Home."

- Go to the bathroom at the end of dinner and bring your coat and handbag. While in the bathroom, take off every stitch of clothing you are wearing and neatly pack it inside your bag. When you return to the table, deliver your handbag to your lover and tell him or her to peek inside. Without words, stand up and unbutton the top button of your coat revealing just enough flesh to hint towards your scandalous surprise.

- Ask your lover to meet you for dinner at a fancy hotel. After dinner, instead of putting down your credit card, place the key to a room you have rented upstairs.

- Ask your lover to meet you at a museum. Before you meet, create a beautiful hand-drawn map of the museum that leads to your favorite exhibits. Tell your lover to lead you on an adventure of fantasy, and when you arrive at each piece, share with each other the fantasies that each piece inspires.

- Pack a sexy fruit in a beautiful container and send them with your lover to work. That day, send photos of the fruit arranged provocatively on a plate, at the market or on your naked body. When she or he arrives home, greet them with the taste of that fruit on your tongue, and see what adventures that nectar inspires next.

- Choose a sexy song with scandalous lyrics. Tell your lover to listen to the lyrics only when he or she is alone, eyes closed. Make her or him hang on every word, and have them write a favorite line on your naked body with melted chocolate.

"Renouncement: the heroism of mediocrity."

— *Natalie Clifford Barney*

CHAPTER 5

THE BODY BEAUTIFUL

> *"The curves of the female*
> *form have the power to stop*
> *a war and start a revolution."*
>
> –Kitty Cavalier

The first time I ever sat down to write a class description about what I teach, the above line was the first thing to spring from my brain through my fingertips. I didn't even know where it came from, but there it was. Little did I know that this line, would and continues to shape my entire life.

How I got started in seduction was through burlesque. As you read in Chapter One, performing burlesque was life altering. Every performance was a transcendent experience for me. Shortly after I began performing, a few girlfriends who had witnessed my transformation accosted me. "You have to teach us how to do that!" they said. I scoffed at the idea.

Who was I to teach burlesque? I was no
expert. I was barely a performer. How
could I teach something I didn't know?

But that's the thing: I did know. We all know. The first time I ever took a lesson with Jo "Boobs" Weldon of the New York School of Burlesque she said these words to me: "flirting, seduction, tease — all of this is already in your DNA. I am not actually here to teach you anything new. I am just showing you how to remember something you already know."

I tossed my coin in the fountain, hunkered down with an album of old jazz tunes and said what the hell. I taught my first burlesque class in a musty, dusty studio on 42nd Street on a hot night in July 2009, and 20 women showed up to have a little of what I was having. The thing they wanted was not perfect technique or outstanding dance ability. They saw a woman who was confident, who loved herself inside and out and was unafraid to express this down to its very core, stripping away, literally, every layer, and exposing all that I was with courage, sass and pride.

That was what they wanted and that was what they got. After class, I couldn't believe my luck. I just got paid to share my greatest joy. Still wearing my costume from class, my eyes sore from being so alert, I spread out their collective $20 entrance fees on my bed and rolled around in it to the song, "Golden", by Jill Scott, ritualistically expressing my gratitude at the privilege of being able to live my journey, inspire others, and be rewarded for it.

After that special day I continued to teach burlesque classes as a means to body love and body empowerment. But eventually I got itchy. While I love burlesque from here to kingdom come, it was not the dance itself that revved my engines the most. It was the action of artistically honoring the Erotic Divine through striptease — which is ultimately a metaphor for the practice of sacred seduction.

In burlesque, having a great costume, stage technique, audience communication and all the other technical elements are important in giving a good show, but this is not a complete formula for fascination. The missing golden ticket is this: contagious ownership of everything you are and unapologetic expression of it.

Based on my experience, this is why on the burlesque stage a person can ace the acrobatics of a performance, but if the ownership, the fun, the sizzle is not there, it leaves the audience with the taste of a very weak cup of tea.

Conversely, if a performer comes out onstage and is there to have the fucking time of her life no matter what that she looks like, she can do something as simple as peel and reveal a glove over and over for a full three minutes and leave the audience mesmerized, salivating, and begging for more. And so it is with sacred seduction. The magic elixir is not a flat stomach or a pair of perky bazooms.

Ownership. Sparkle. Sizzle. That is the key.

It is my belief that one of the cornerstones of our sense of ownership is how we relate to our feminine form. Our bodies are Goddess in the flesh, Aphrodite on Earth. The curve of our lips, the sway of our hips, the feel of our skin, the point of our chin — these are the things that churches, temples and all other houses of worship seek to imitate. The more we can own the perfection of our imperfections, the more divine we look and feel.

Tell the girdle to go fuck itself.
Realness is the new dreamgirl.

THERE IS NO SUCH THING AS "THE PERFECT BODY"

One of the most undeniable virtues of a true Sacred Seductress is the way she loves her flesh. A Seductress loves every inch of herself: smooth skin, dimpled skin, parts that stick out, parts that just don't. It is all as beautiful as a sunrise to her. And because of the conviction in her self-love, the judgments one usually makes about a female body seem to slip away when he or she is in her presence. She is that powerful.

A Seductress does not wait around for the "perfect body" to arrive in order to feel and know her full sensual and erotic power. The things she is told she should be ashamed of (fat on her belly, one breast that is smaller than the other, her skin tone, etc.), she flaunts rather than hides like the diamonds that they are: rare, beautiful and perfectly imperfect.

The way a woman feels about her body is a mirror image to what she believes about herself, her Divinity, and how she relates to the world. Body hatred is an epidemic amongst women. We live in a culture that teaches us to believe that we must meet an impossible list of qualifications in order to feel "beautiful".

The tricky thing about this list of benchmarks, however, is that there is not a woman alive who could even come close to meeting them all. For every woman who wishes her hips were smaller, there is a woman who wishes her hips were more round. For every woman who wishes her breasts were fuller, there is a woman wishing she could wear T-shirts without feeling self-conscious. It reminds me of the story "The Emperor's New Clothes". We are all striving so desperately to be perfect, sexy, beautiful, young; and yet it is this exact desperation to change what is already perfect that makes us all feel so downright ugly.

A Seductress transcends this (forgive me) mind-fuck by making the important distinction between true beauty, and the illusion of "learned beauty". Learned beauty is what we do when our sole purpose is to gain the approval of others. It is living by the message of what we have been taught beautiful means, rather than the beauty that we know is true in our soul.

When we aim to achieve the beauty we have learned, we are dependent on external validation to convince us of our power and radiance. But a true Seductress knows with every fiber of her being that her beauty has nothing to do with her lip gloss. Her lip gloss can be a lovely expression of her beauty, but it is certainly not the source of it.

True beauty is eternal. It never leaves us. It does not change with our outfit or our hairstyle or our age. True beauty means that we need never pause in the mirror and ask ourselves, "Do I look beautiful right now?", because true beauty needs never be questioned. It is a simple feminine truth.

IMAGES THAT MAKE YOU FEEL GOOD

Furnish your home with images that make you feel good about your body.

I love to look at images of other bodies that look like mine. Renaissance paintings, Crystal Renn high fashion photo spreads and just seeing other bodies that resemble mine remind me that my body is actually normal, gorgeous and just right.

BUT WHAT ABOUT BEING HEALTHY KITTY?

Often when a person is exposed to this philosophy, particularly if they are new to it, they jump to the health implications involved in prying our body dissatisfaction out of our white-knuckled fingers. It's almost as if by loving our bodies as is rather than striving for imagined perfection, we are afraid we will lose the drive to take care of ourselves.

Easy now. I'm not trying to take away anyone's Omega 3s. All I'm trying to say is this: You cannot fix abuse with more abuse.

One of my favorite books/movies of all time is "Little Women." In one scene, Amy, the youngest of the four girls, runs home after school with bloody hands after being beaten for disorderly conduct. Susan Sarandon's character, Marmee, Amy's mother, is livid. In a letter to the teacher she states, "What right have you to strike a child? In God's eyes, we are all children, and we are all equals. If you hit and humiliate a child, the only lesson she will learn is to hit and humiliate."

This is exactly how I feel about body image. For the first 25 years of my life I tried as hard as I could to beat my body into submission. I thought if I could crest the mountain of self-hatred high enough I would someday have an a-ha moment that would finally motivate me to change my ways and become a fitness queen. I really thought that my self-destructive thoughts and behaviors were actually good for me.

But as we know, like attracts like. If you strike and beat a dog, will it come eat out of the palm of your hand? If you take an abused child who is acting out in school, is the answer to hit them harder? Abuse begets abuse. Love begets love. My attitude of finding our bodies perfect no matter what the size, shape or cholesterol count is not a way to check out. Quite the opposite. It is a way to check all the way in. To quote Mitch Albom, "Love wins, love always wins."

BOGGARTS

When women look at me, my hope is that they see a woman who takes pride in everything that she is, body and soul. I seek to hold the space for radical acceptance and the flaunting of flaws.

But there are days where I feel fat. And ugly. There are still times where I overeat to soothe myself, and times where I zip up my dress before a date, and if it feels loose I feel powerful, if it feels tight I feel repellent.

What's a girl to do here?

I have invested many years of my life, not to mention many thousands of dollars, working to heal my outlook on my body. I have done so with great success. As a woman who couldn't bear to wear short sleeves in the summer for fear of exposing my upper arm flesh who has transformed into a curve-flaunting burlesque dancer, I don't have much to complain about.

And yet, those moments of self-doubt and self-hatred still occur. Does that mean it was all awash? Does it mean I should just work HARDER to heal, dammit? With either of these approaches I am left swimming upstream.

So I decide to just see them for what they are: boggarts.

In the book, "Harry Potter and the Prisoner of Azkaban," there is a scene in class where Harry is being taught how to defend himself against a dark, destructive magical creature called a boggart.

A boggart is a shapeshifting spirit that has the ability to turn into whatever is your greatest fear. Open the cabinet door on a boggart and you might find an enormous spider darting at you with deadly pincers, your high school teacher that would look the other way on wedgies, or even the body of a dead loved one.

That's kind of what it feels like during those moments of body image anxiety. A belly peeking out farther than flat can become the reason you are still single. Flailing arm flab harkens to your inability to discipline yourself, explaining why you are underpaid and still in debt, going nowhere. Thick thighs become the very thing that stands in the way of gaining your parents' love and approval. It's not only fat, but wrinkles on your face, dark circles under your eyes, boobs that are well endowed, but not perky enough, toes that are too stubby or too long; anything that makes us feel that paralyzing sense of feminine insecurity can be considered a boggart. How they appear is not actually real. It is the belief that they are real that gives them their power.

> *"The ugly may be beautiful,*
> *the pretty never."*
> — *Paul Gauguin*

A woman who is able to see the beauty in her flesh no matter what the circumstances contains enormous power. When she can see the beauty in the whole mosaic, not just the individual tiles, there is nothing — no stigma, no scare tactic and no insult that can ever mess with the strength of her radiance.

Knowing this is very liberating. It means that in moments of insecurity — when you have a visible panty line, when your belly is peeking out over the top of your jeans, when you are wearing a bathing suit and you forgot to shave your bikini line — you have an instant cure for that which is making you lose your head.

If you own it, rock it; act like it is the sexiest thing about you, suddenly that is what it becomes. It is not how others perceive us that sets the dial on our magnetism.

To own something means it belongs to you. It is a part of you. How you own it is you claim it, you make it yours. If you feel like you can't, act as if. Imagine you are a world-renowned artist and you have been given permission to view the most inspiring object ever to grace the planet: your own legs. Or hips. Or belly. Or breasts.

When you look through the eyes of appreciation, what do you see?

ADORATION

A Poem by Kitty Cavalier

I adore My Body.
It is so scrumptious and delicious, I just want to gobble myself up.

I love my legs. They are like the most elegant champagne flutes. I imagine that if they were a food, they would taste like lady fingers drizzled with chocolate and whipped cream.

I love my arms. I love the way they taper delicately at the wrist. I love their shape as I hold onto the subway rail. I love the way my muscles flex as I sway from side to side.

I love my breasts, they are like the ripest plum, hanging on a vine in Tuscany, warm from the sun.

I adore my hips. Their curves, the way I can grab the flesh on the bone. They give me a sense of home, like a crisp, brown Christmas turkey cooked with butter under the skin. Yum.

I love my belly. I love the roundness of it. I love the density of it. I love how it stands by me, day after day. I love how authentically feminine it is. I love having it massaged in a warm bath with oil underwater. I love how the Goddess lives in my belly, my center, my strength.

I LOVE my shoulders, my clavicle, and my decollete. My clavicle is like an Olympic ice skater. Graceful, elegant. A perfect 10. My decollete, smooth like the frosting on top of a birthday cake. My shoulders, like the pillars in the Sistine Chapel, holding everything together with strength, grace and beauty.

I love my tresses. Like warm amber honey. Smooth, lustrous, sensuous. Perfect on their own, but also the perfect complement to my gorgeous face.

I love my face. My eyes, like looking down an endless beach. My lips, like perfect velvet pillows you just want to sink into. My skin, like the creamy froth on top of a cappuccino.

I love being a woman.
I love being me.
In the words of Doris Day, "I enjoy being a girl".

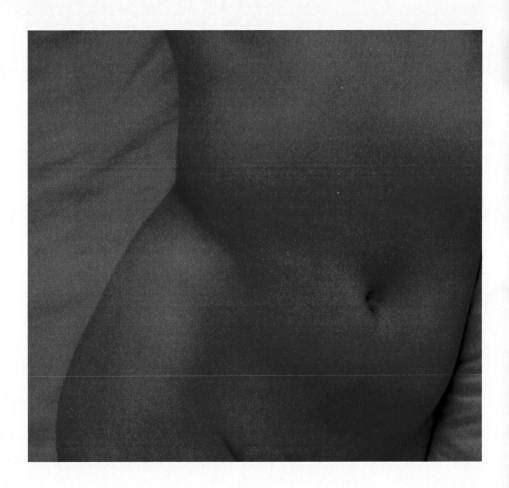

THE

APPRECIATION MIRROR

Choose one mirror in your home
to be the appreciation mirror.

The rule is: whenever you pass by that mirror you must choose to see what you love rather than what you can criticize. Mirrors are taught to be devices of torture for women. We zero in on what we can improve rather than what we can appreciate. Take this one mirror and make it like a big glass window onto a beautiful view of the horizon. Except this time, rather than looking out, you are looking in to be brought to rapture by what you see.

*"People will stare. Make
it worth their while."*

— *Harry Winston*

Gucci.

Prada.

Neolithic woman.

When it comes to ornamenting ourselves, we meet a mix of excitement and exhaustion, the see-saw of which dips back and forth from day to day. The experience of dressing up can be galvanizing and enlivening.

But sometimes, the pressure to be fashionable can be draining and competitive.

With all the money we spend on clothes, makeup, etc., and the way it contributes to the global condition of feminine insecurity, well, it's enough to make you want to burn your bra, your lipstick; even the hair off your head.

What then, is the point of dressing up?

Well, like most things with seduction, there is more to the story than what we have been told.

"If anything is sacred, the human body is sacred."

— Walt Whitman

When our ancestors would show up to ceremony around the fire on the night of a full moon, they would not appear in some mud-encrusted, tattered frock they had been wearing for weeks. They would bathe for DAYS, massage themselves and each other with fragranced oil and herbal salves. Their faces would be painted. Their wrists, ankles, necks and heads would be adorned with fine shells and earth gems.

They clearly demonstrated that beauty is a form of reverence and prayer, and that when Spirit itself is your Friday night date, you damn well better get your glow on.

When a person gets married, she or he will spend up to a year on improving her or his appearance. When you show up to a job interview, you make sure you look like you have your shit together — and then some — on the inner and the outer.

Adorning ourselves is just another way to increase the wattage on the vibrancy of our light. Accentuating our lips, outlining our eyes, wearing shoes that dazzle, adding luster to our hair; these are all totems that represent our inner-made manifest on the outer.

When dressing and adorning, it is easy to fall into the trap of painting to please the voyeur, rather than for the pleasure of making art. Who are we trying to please/impress? Boyfriends? Girlfriends? Colleagues? Bosses? Our parents? Our kids?

Hold it right there, lady. Remember that ornamentation is not about impressing the Joneses, it is about impressing upon the world the magic and uniqueness that is YOU.

Ornamentation doesn't mean you need to parade the streets in a gilded carriage. (Unless ya want to! I know I do!) It can be as simple as switching your sneakers from regular tennis shoes to a pair of pink Chuck Taylor's. As with everything in sacred seduction: It is not the thing itself, it is the intention behind it that counts.

MAKEUP: A LOVE STORY

"Beauty without expression is boring."

– Ralph Waldo Emerson

Once I was working in an office building and there was a small fire in the floor above us. No one's safety was at risk, but when I heard the firemen were considering evacuation, my mind immediately went to one place: my makeup. That may sound vain, but to me, makeup is very sacred.

I regard makeup the same way artists regard their paint and brushes. I don't wear makeup because I feel I have to; I wear it because I want to. I take so much pleasure from creating art in this way and sharing it with the world.

I love making my lips look like they just had a good make-out session, my eyes look like a Cape Cod sunset. I love having the ability to invoke the bronze glow of summer right in the heart of winter. I love being able to imitate and honor the Femme Vitales I idolize. I love the ritual of getting ready with girlfriends.

Some of the fondest memories of my teenage years are my best friend, Becca, and I parked in some parking lot in our small town, covering up our adolescent blemishes as we bared our tender, newly discovered souls. I consider makeup to be a feminine rite.

I remember my 13th birthday, knowing I was truly a teenager when I received a Caboodles case full of bold shades from the drugstore. I remember buying my first big-girl lipstick at age 15 (Ecru by Lancome) for a whole $17. I remember the tissues that littered my Mother's purse, all covered in big frosty pink kisses.

When I am feeling low makeup lifts me up, brings me back to level. It is the one thing I can count on to make me feel fabulous, always. Makeup deeply nourishes my soul. Have fun as you decorate the canvas of you — a living work of art!

"Taking joy in living is a woman's best cosmetic."

Rosalind Russell

"The happiest girls are the prettiest."

Audrey Hepburn

"Beauty is unbearable, drives us to despair, offering us for a minute the glimpse of an eternity that we should like to stretch out over the whole of time."

Albert Camus

"Beauty is not caused. It is."

Emily Dickinson

"Beauty is a form of Genius — is higher, indeed, than Genius, as it needs no explanation."

Oscar Wilde

"Let the soft animal of your body love what it loves."

Mary Oliver

"I don't need a bedroom to prove my womanliness. I can convey just as much sex appeal, picking apples off a tree or standing in the rain."

Audrey Hepburn

"Sex appeal is fifty percent what you've got and fifty percent what people think you've got."

Sophia Loren

CHAPTER 6

THE FEMME
FATALE

> *"Trouble needs a home girls,*
> *will you give her one?"*
>
> — *Tori Amos*

Salome.
Mata Hari.
Delilah.
Cleopatra.
Circe.

All of them legendary. All of them dangerous. All of them power-ful. All of them Femme Fatales. The Femme Fatale is an archetypal and literary character whose presence can be felt in stories as early as the Old Testament. She is a woman with keen sexual prowess who uses this ancient power to her own behest. Her powers of attrac-tion override the logic-based society in which we live, which is what makes her so dangerous and threatening. She is fierce, opinionated, bad ass and smart as a whip. She is a feather ruffler and a wave maker. She enjoys conflict not just for sport, but because she sees it as a necessary component to expansion for herself, her community and her world.

Femme Fatale literally translated means "fatal woman". When approached with fear, this sounds like a monster to be avoided, but when acknowledged with consciousness, we can see that this is just another side of the sacred seductress. The femme fa-tale is not a type of woman, it is an element to our womanhood. The femme fatale befriends death — the death of relationships, behavior patterns, etc. — in service to creating life. She is fierce about her boundaries and says exactly what is on her mind.

She is wild and uncontained. Rather than exploit her powers of attraction, she lives them unapologetically.

> *"When my enemies stop hissing,*
> *I will know that I am slipping."*
>
> — *Maria Callas*

Let's examine one of the most notorious seductresses of all time and her legacy of legend, Cleopatra. Cleopatra is a legend of a seductress whose tale has survived since 30BC.

You may know some of her epic tales, like sneaking into the suite of Julius Caesar by hiding inside a rolled up carpet and revealing herself as the magnificent carpet was unfurled. Or perhaps you heard the story of the first time she met Mark Antony, when in true diva fashion, while Mark Antony was waiting for her to come to him, she seduced all of Rome down to the riverbank, including Antony himself.

On a ship with purple sails soaked in fine perfume and her crew dressed as golden nymphs, Mark Antony could not help but give up his pride, stop waiting, and go to her instead.

Cleopatra is well-known for her kohl-rimmed eyes, milk baths and other feminine wiles. But what we often forget is that she was also one of the most influential and prolific political leaders in the history of the world.

What I love about Cleopatra's conquests is how they beautifully demonstrate a quality found in all great seductresses of power: She was inclusive of her erotic power, rather than dismissive of it. She would often dress to channel the Goddess Isis, mother of death and rebirth. Her sensuality was her ally, not her enemy. In our culture today, this is seen as "using your sexuality to get something", a horrifying offense if ever there was one. But I urge you to take a second look.

Cleopatra was not manipulative, she was simply uncensored. She was true to herself and her authenticity. She made no at-

tempt to conform to a boys club. She remained totally herself, simply loving whatever and whomever she wanted, and by virtue, was unstoppable.

A femme fatale knows what she wants when she wants it. She is not afraid to get shit done.

She is often painted as a damaged, broken bird that is out to get the men who scorned her, only furthering her torrent of tears. Not so in the paradigm of sacred seduction. Let's take a look at some other dames whose anger, frustration and subsequent courage have forever altered the world in which we live.

"When I'm good, I'm very good. But when I'm bad I'm better."

—*Mae West*

FEMME FATALES

Martha Gellhorn

Known as "the blonde peril", Martha Gellhorn was the first female war correspondent and an acclaimed journalist. Growing up in St. Louis, Missouri, with a family of three brothers and parents who encouraged having strong opinions, Ms. Gellhorn was a filly bursting from the gate, a force to be reckoned with in a male-dominated world.

A seductress of legend who was married thrice (once to the formidable Ernest Hemingway), her achievements and the way she changed the world of journalism for women make her a one-woman revolution. *Rock on Martie, rock on.*

Josephine Baker

Josephine Baker is perhaps most well-known for her feathers, her bananas, her grapes and all the other accoutrements that made her career as an entertainer remarkable. Josephine was raised in St. Louis, in the early 1900s. In 1925, fed up with the racial inequality in America, Josephine traveled to Paris to perform in a burlesque/cabaret revue. She made quite the impression. Earning the admiration of Paris public figures, including E.E. Cummings, Hemingway and Pablo Picasso, she denied more than a thousand marriage proposals.

A femme fatale for her subversiveness to start, Josephine let her real bad-ass, bully-busting bitch out to play during WWII.

From biography.com:

Baker worked for the Red Cross during the occupation of France. As a member of the Free French forces she also entertained troops in both Africa and the Middle East. Perhaps most importantly, however, Baker did work for the French Resistance, at times smuggling messages hidden in her sheet music and even in her underwear. For these efforts, at the war's end, Baker was awarded both the Croix de Guerre and the Legion of Honour with the rosette of the Resistance, two of France's highest military honors.

Lilith

Did you know that Adam had a first wife before the lovely Eve? More she-wolf than subservient, Lilith was downright OVER IT when it came to God's wagging finger. Fed up with Adam's fearful unwillingness to ravage and savage her in the delights of sex, she willingly left the Garden of Eden to descend to the underworld. There she received every orgiastic endeavor a girl could ask for. Of course, because she symbolized a powerful woman with unbridled lust, legend twisted her fate into being a fire-breathing demon that goes around stealing the breath of babies in the night. (I wonder if this is where those Disney movies get their inspiration for the Evil Queens?) Mess with the lust, you get the horns, boys.

It is easy to look back on these babes and applaud their accolades now that enough time has passed for their actions to have positively altered our reality. But at the time, can you imagine the names they must have been called?

Crazy bitch
Selfish
Insatiable
Hysterical
Shrew
Demanding
Irrational
Over-reactive
Emotional
Bipolar
Banshee
Man-haters
Aggressive
Unladylike

The secret to a femme fatale being a force of positive change is that she takes all these labels and owns them as being right rather than wrong. When you look at all the inequality, violence and oppression that exists in the world, you are damn right we are driven to be banshee bitches ready to fight.

In the realm of sacred seduction however, a femme fatale starts fire around which to gather rather than burning down the house. She uses her feelings of dissatisfaction, anger, betrayal, grief and bitterness as the Miracle-Gro for the change she wishes to see.

Join me as we step into the parlor, take off her centuries-old muzzle, hand her a microphone and let her be heard.

PARLOR GAME

THE

FEMME FATALE

HONOR THAT CRAZY BITCH

Just for funsies, let's indulge your crazy bitch. Write out all the things that you think make you crazy.

Examples would be:

- Sometimes I hate my children.

- I wish I could just pack up and leave my life.

- My cube mate at work is so fat and that makes me hate her.

- My cube mate at work is so skinny and that makes me hate her.

- I wish my mother would die.

- My life sucks so much I wish I was never born.

- There is genocide happening and all I can think about is how many french fries I had at lunch.

If you're feeling really brave, share these thoughts with your Seduction Society. Knowing that you are not alone in having these thoughts and feelings is the antidote to the way they can plague and paralyze you.

When we can share collectively that this is a global insanity, we realize that it is so not personal. We are not bad for having these thoughts, they are just symptoms of the bigger problem: our oppression. Taking off the shroud that is trying to keep them hidden makes space for new thoughts to emerge.

Then, take your list and ceremonially burn it or bury it in the earth. This is not to get rid of the things on your list, it is to ritualistically transform them. Turn on an awesome song and dance to honor your inner Femme Fatale, that bad ass bitch that sees discord and is unafraid to speak up, and act up. Even if you feel like you can't imagine being able to honor her, dance your willingness to be willing.

Sometimes things piss us off and we don't even realize it. For three days in a row, keep a diary of all the things that anger you. Run the gamut — miniscule to massive. Awareness is always the first step to taking action.

Create Art of the Change You Wish to Make

As you become aware of your feelings of anger, frustration, sadness and grief, the other side of that coin is inspiration to make a change. What is it you want to see more of in this world? Freedom? Equality? Forgiveness? Kindness? Pleasure? Joy? Make a collage, an altar, even a detail in your daily outfit that plants the seed of expression. Art creates beauty. Beauty creates healing. Healing creates a better world.

Experiment With Saying Exactly What Is on Your Mind

One day, I decided that just for the hell of it, I was going to say exactly what was on my mind to people I didn't know. You know what happened? Not much. Often we think that by asking for what we really want or saying what we really think we are being too much. But the truth is, too much of you is really just enough.

THE TEMPTRESS

As honor worthy as the Femme Fatale/Seductress archetype may be, we would be fools to deny that seduction, like all things, has a shadow side that is a force to be reckoned with. Seduction gets a reputation for being a craft of manipulative wrongdoing. Right here, right now, let's dance with the diva of divine seductive darkness herself: The Temptress.

*"Well-behaved women
seldom make history."*

– Laurel Thatcher Ulrich

One of my favorite movies that articulates the difference between sacred, surrender-driven seduction and fear-based, manipulative seduction is "The Sound of Music." Maria von Trapp,
talk about a legend of sacred seduction. She inspires the other
nuns to write songs about her and her wild spirit. She is able to
tame the untamable by meeting the von Trapp children on their
level — through play, song and silliness, but never compromising
on her values just to gain their approval. Then, of course, there is
the spell she casts on Captain von Trapp. She becomes irresistible
to him simply by surrendering to her wild, wide open heart day
after day.

In stark contrast, we are also presented with the opposite side of
the spectrum: Baroness Schraeder. As Captain von Trapp's fiancée,
she is depicted as the classic bombshell with a golden spade in her
pocket, ready to dig for gold the minute he turns his back. With
her priorities set solely on progressing in society, she is disinterested in the children and intends to send them to boarding school
as soon as she and the captain say "I do." She is, in other words,
The Temptress.

I actually love the term temptress and it has many positive con-
notations in the realm of seduction, but in this context we are using it to describe a woman with an appetite for control, impulsive
satisfaction and senseless destruction.

What I am referring to here is a classic example of that type of
seductress who looks sweet as tupelo honey on the outside, but

is so hardened inside that trying to take a bite would break your molars in half.

Let's take a little inventory. Have you ever:

- Gone shopping and spent way more than you wanted to, regretting your purchase and feeling bad about yourself afterwards?

- Sent a text to an ex that you regret?

- Pigged out to the point of nausea, or starved yourself to the point of depletion?

- Used your power over someone just because you knew you could?

- Manipulated someone by pushing their buttons because you knew you could?

Sound familiar?

Of course you have, we all have. The reason is that within us all is the sacred seductress/temptress dichotomy. Having a tendency toward the temptress does not make us stupid, evil or wrong. It makes us deeply human and perfectly imperfect.

The reason I choose to use the word "temptress" is because while temptation can be pleasurable when given in proper doses, it can be wildly unpleasurable when it is experienced as a constant. Living in a constant state of temptation without being able to become satisfied no matter how much you consume is a horrible state in which to be.

What breeds this part of ourselves into being? Why is the temptress such a pain-in-the-ass scallywag out to ruin our experience of sacred seduction? Careful now. It makes sense that we would want to shake her off like an annoying little sister who makes us look uncool and trashes our image. But when dealing with the temptress, the most important thing to remember is this:

Our ability to show compassion to the Temptress is in direct proportion to our ability to succeed in living a life of sacred seduction.

The reason? The temptress in us is not evil by nature. She is deeply wounded by a culture that has sought to annihilate her natural seductive powers and violated her sense of self at every turn. Because women have been and continue to be violated on a daily basis through acts of violence both physical (rape occurs every 11 seconds in the U.S.) and psychological (media messages) not to mention having our existence fundamentally socially invalidated ("all men are created equal") well, golly, it makes me want to start a riot! When looked at from this perspective, it is easy and righteous to see why the Temptress has such a ravenous appetite for destruction.

In the 2014 State of the Union address, President Obama quoted that women earn 77 cents for every dollar a man makes. That's 23 flipping percent! What would you do if for every dollar you received in change after shopping at the grocery store you got a 23-cent bonus? What would you do with all that spare change? Take a vacation and get some rest from the litany of things that are expected of you on a daily basis as a woman? Do something philanthropic and create positive change in the world, like regulating food subsidies so our children are not dying of chemical-related diseases while CEOs puff-puff on their cigars? Or maybe you would invest it, yielding interest and growing your financial security so that you wouldn't have to work 123 hours to every 100 hours your male colleagues work to make the same amount. That's 23 extra hours you get to spend enjoying your kids, writing, going for bike rides, making sumptuous meals for your closest friends or having soul-quaking, passionate sex.

Twenty-three cents is a big fucking deal, people.

So it makes sense that the temptress is living out a legacy of scarcity and trying to consume everything in her path. She's been starved out for too long and she will take what's hers by any means necessary. The problem is, she has been so hungry for so long that she has no way of regulating her appetite. Like a tornado, she could consume an entire house, an entire town, an entire city, and still never get her fix.

In "The Sound of Music" there is one powerful scene during which the baroness catches Maria and the captain dancing innocently under the stars. Threatened and panicked about the potential loss of security she has been working so hard to build, she corners Maria at a vulnerable moment and pretends to be her friend and ally, meanwhile planting bombs like "there is nothing more irresistible to a man than a woman who's in love with him" and "you were blushing in his arms".

Out of shame and humiliation, as well as a silent resonance with these statements being true, Maria flees the von Trapp home, leaving behind the children, the man, and the life she loves.

In this story line, however, the power of sacred seduction takes hold. The captain's feelings for Maria are too intense to be denied, and in seeing this the baroness decides to save face and break it off with him before he can hurt her. As she exits gracefully, leaving the captain with a slight smile on her lips, she turns away and we see past the façade into her internal world as her smile fades and falls.

So what then is to be done? Remember, trying to shirk the Temptress will only strengthen her resolve. You cannot fix abuse with more abuse. A sacred seductress is a woman who owns herself head to toe. This means that there is no part to her mosaic that is invaluable. The dull clay that holds things together is just as precious and gorgeous as the glittering ceramic tiles.

TEASING OUT
THE TEMPTRESS

Close your eyes and take a deep breath. Envision a figure walking towards you. As it comes closer, you see that it is your inner Temptress come to life. Invite her to take a seat. Look into her eyes. Notice what she is wearing. When you are ready, ask her, "What is it that you need?" Receive her answer, even if she has nothing to say. Then ask her, "Is there anything else you would like me to know?"

Receive her answer again. When you feel complete, give her a nice, big, long hug, and watch her walk away.

Write one page in your seduction diary about what she had to tell you.

The only thing to be done is this: We must draw her into our lap, coo into her ear, stroke her hair, and tell her everything is going to be just fine. Why is everything going to be okay? You are going to make it so. Yes, you.

If the Femme Fatale seductresses were here they would tell us it is time to grow a set girls — of ovaries, that is. As women, we have greater social and economic power than ever before. It's time to light the fire in our bellies, paw at the ground and take off running. It's time to own it all.

Then open your eyes and write her a letter. The object is not to write things perfectly, it is simply to let your consciousness stream out onto the page. If we let her, the Temptress has enormous wisdom to offer. Listen closely, and she will teach you a lot.

〜

SEDUCTIVE ASSERTIVENESS

"Only let us be thankful that the darlings [women] are like the beasts of the field, and don't know their own power. They would overcome us entirely if they did."

— *William Makepeace Thackeray*

Imagine with me, if you will, the following scenarios:

You are finally done with work after an extremely long day and you are on your way to pick up your kids. It is 4 p.m. and you barely have it in you to pick up a roast chicken from the grocery store.

You are looking forward to an evening of having a simple dinner, and early bedtime and a private bubble bath with a new book that enthralls you. Not only are you looking forward to this — you depend on it. On your way to the school you get a text from your neighbor saying that she is stuck at work and could you please take her kids home with you until she is free?

What the hell. You get it. You've been stuck at work with a kid dilemma before. Why not pay a few shillings forward in the karmic bank.

Fast forward to 6 p.m. You suddenly have five kids on your hands who are hyper as hell and this staying late at work has turned into a "massive project-late night" affair.

In your resentment and dissatisfaction, you have a few choices for handling this situation:

1. You text "no problem" to your neighbor and pack up your desire of a relaxing night to yourself into a tiny square that would rival a master of miniature origami. **(PASSIVE)**

2. You text "ok, let me know when you are on your way" to your neighbor. Then you feed the kids gummy bears and french fries for dinner and let them watch TV until their eyeballs are ready to fall out. **(PASSIVE AGGRESSIVE)**

3. You call your neighbor and rage about how you have a life and she should take more responsibility for her kids. Oh, and by the way, her kids need a serious bath, FYI. **(AGGRESSIVE)**

4. In the moment you receive the initial text from your neighbor, you let her know you would love to help but you are not available this evening. You ask, "Is there another way I can help you figure

this out?" thereby honoring her needs but not sacrificing your own. **(ASSERTIVE)**

In *The Assertiveness Workbook*, author Randy J. Paterson states: "Assertiveness isn't about building a good disguise. It's about developing the courage to take the disguise off. [This workbook is for] the ones who have already tried wearing a mask and have found they can't breathe very well with it on. They want to go out into the world naked faced, as themselves, but not defenseless. They want to be themselves in a way that doesn't push others off-stage. In a way that invites the people they meet to be more fully themselves too."

I love this book and I love this paragraph. It speaks directly to why assertiveness is in fact so seductive. There are few things more alluring to the positive and repellent to the negative, than honestly, humbly, transparently speaking one's truth.

Seems so simple, right? Simple, but not always easy.

If seductive assertiveness is clearly the most constructive and positive option listed above, why does it often feel so difficult to speak our truth in the moment?

Well, let's examine what would have happened 100, 500 or 5,000 years ago if a woman unabashedly embraced her truth, going against the grain of obligatory servitude that had been culturally set out for her.

Burning at the stake
Being stoned to death
Imprisonment
Abolishment and isolation from the community

Just for starters. This is not just history, this is present day. Forget 5,000 years. We encounter these atrocities every day when a woman steps out of line in the eyes of a culture that dominates her, in the news, in our communities, in our very own homes.

After such a history of having to stuff our true feelings down, we have become masters of manipulation when it comes to hiding our true thoughts and intentions. Often this is not even conscious. In the moment we say, "yes", without really consulting our deepest truth. We may not even realize until after the decision has been made that we performed a spiritual bypass on how we really feel in order to keep ourselves in line with what is expected of us.

The result is a bottling of tension and anger that becomes so potent, so intense, that we feel like we run the risk of belching out a fireball in the simple act of refusing sugar in our tea. The consequence becomes much greater than "yes" or "no". It feels like if we really allow ourselves to feel our truth, just by opening our mouths, we could set someone's hair on fire, not to mention our very own house!

The practice of seductive assertiveness is exactly that. It is a practice. I have burned a lot of bridges in order to understand and gauge my own firepower. It is only in trying out every setting on the dial that I have been able to master the heat setting on which to cook up great communication.

The following exercise is meant to be done over and over for the refinement of your expertise in the art of seductive assertiveness. (It is a variation on an exercise called "assertiveness scorecards" in *The Assertiveness Workbook*, which I highly recommend.)

SEDUCTIVE ASSERTIVENESS

DATE:

PLACE:

PERSON:

WHAT HAPPENED:

HOW DO YOU FEEL ABOUT
YOUR RESPONSE?

HOW MIGHT YOU HANDLE
THIS SITUATION DIFFERENTLY
IN THE FUTURE?

*Think of this exercise as a golden permission slip
to cross the border lines of saying what is true.*

There really is no way to do this wrong when your intention is to simply become a more graceful communicator. I recommend doing this exercise when big things happen, but perhaps more importantly, when little things happen. When big things happen, the swell of emotion is sometimes so great that it easily activates our instincts, giving us clear direction on what action we need to take to be carried to shore. The little things, on the other hand, are far more insidious. But like a stack of kindling that just keeps building, these are the makings of a bonfire. Pay attention and play this game as often as you like to refine your ability to speak your truth with elegance, poise and grace.

SIN BIGGER SINS

*"When I'm good, I'm very good,
but when I'm bad I'm better."*

—*Mae West*

I grew up a good Catholic girl. But not just any good Catholic girl — a "my children's Bible never left my side" kind of good Catholic girl. I perfected my prayers like a ballerina would practice pirouettes. I loved Lent, sacrifice and suffering for others. At age 7, I thought my future life would be a choice between two costumes : a nun's habit or Mom jeans.

My parents were the somewhat progressive, guitar mass kind of Catholics. Growing up in a town of a thousand people, church and religion was one of the only places where I felt like I was part of the "in" crowd. With a set of rules I could follow I had a formula for living a good, worthy life. I could go to Church, say the prayers, kneel on the kneelers while keeping my butt off the seat, and all of it offered me validation I so desperately craved. It was a way I could measure whether or not I was doing things "right".

In preparation for the sacrament of penance, we were instructed to learn a prayer called the Act of Contrition. I remember reciting these words: "I firmly intend, with God's help, to do penance, to sin no more, and to avoid whatever leads me to sin."

Those were the words that fell from my lips, but shamefully my head revolted against this litany. "But I like sinning!" I said to myself, "Sinning is the only time I have any fun! I'll die if I can't sin!"

I was suddenly met with the conflict of deeply enjoying the act of sin. Masturbation, yelling back at my parents when I got mad, sneaking cookies from the cookie jar; these were just some of the things that I knew I couldn't live with, but also knew I couldn't live without.

As I got older, so did the stakes. Practicing making out with my teddy bear became actually making out with boys. Talking back to my parents became staying out until 3 a.m. without calling to let them know where I was. The cookie jar? A drink or a joint at a party.

For a long time I would beat myself up for all the sins I had committed in my life, all the mistakes I made. Looking back now, I feel no need for forgiveness. I've realized that every "sin" I've ever committed was actually a divine act of trying to find myself and follow my curiosity toward what felt good. Which ironically is when I would find myself feeling closest to what we all call God.

When I learned about sin, it felt like someone was standing 30 feet away from the edge of a cliff saying, "Here is the edge, so do not go beyond this point." My sins were a way of finding out for myself just where that edge really was. Sometimes, I had to go right up to the edge, where I could hear the echo of pebbles bouncing down the canyon as they shifted under my feet. Sometimes it meant getting a running start and swan diving straight into the heart of darkness that lay in the crevasse below.

All these experiments led to some truly gorgeous war wounds, as well as a collection of the most beautiful, mystical, alive moments of my life.

Today, I feel just as close to God as I did when I was 7. Where there used to be an image of a man in a white robe wagging his finger and shaking his head, there now lives a wrinkly old Vegas showgirl, still in her costume, rockin' it even harder than she did in her so-called prime. She wags her finger at me too. But instead of saying, "Don't you dare," she narrows her eyes as she lights her cigarette shouting, "What the hell are you waiting for girlie? Go get 'em!"

CHAPTER 7

SEDUCTION IS SURRENDER

*One night, I adorably tried to teach a
tele-class about how to seduce a lover.*

Tried is the operative word here. It's not that this is a topic I know nothing about. I have had some incredible, romantic, "April in Paris" style love affairs, and I am an artist when it comes to expressing affection. It's not that I failed at the tele-class; it's just that it didn't turn out exactly as I had anticipated.

Before the class I read books and watched TED talks on sex and desire to prepare myself. As the questions started rolling in, I found myself doing little more than parroting my beloved experts. I felt uncomfortable and awkward. I wasn't connecting with the people attending the class. I was trying to give them the answers they wanted to hear rather than what I really thought.

About 15 minutes into the class, I became fed up with the tightness in my throat that came from speaking from my head and not my heart. I confessed on the call, "Everyone, I need to switch gears. I have to admit, I scheduled this class because I think that there should be more in my work about the traditional things we identify with seduction: rose petals, lingerie, walks on the beach and dates in dark secluded corners.

The truth is, it is not my style to start there. Seduction goes way deeper for me than a collection of romantic accessories. Your questions are validating for me that exactly what you want from me is what I have to offer. A way of connecting to your seductive power that is based in having a spiritual love affair with yourself first, then inviting others, should you please. So I'm just going to be myself now, ok?" Everyone laughed and affirmed that was indeed what they came to the class for in the first place.

This was an excellent lesson for me in the art of seductive surrender. My original approach in teaching the class was to pretend I had all the answers and play the authority. That felt uncomfortable and untrue, and there was little to no connection to my students.

When I gave up the idea of how I thought I should be and surrendered to who I really am, the class lit up. Everything flowed, we got to go deep, and we connected to what was really going on beneath the surface of it all. I received e-mails afterward from students saying that they got exactly what they came for, even though they didn't even really know why they came in the first place. "Funny" I responded, "Neither did I!"

Surrender, like most things, is a practice. There was certainly a time where I would have fought tooth and nail to try to mold myself into the kind of seduction teacher I thought I should be. I would have probably left that class feeling horrible about myself, resigning to change everything about how I teach. But after many, many, experiences of practicing seductive surrender, I have learned that it is a lot easier and a lot more effective to just simply go with the flow.

In this chapter, we will explore this essential and enlightening path to the art of embodying the sacred, surrendered seductress.

REJECTION IS PROTECTION

I remember when my best friend, Vivi, was interviewing for a job that we thought was meant to be *her* job. She had interviewed at multiple places that were not the right fit. This job paid a shit ton and she was perfect for it. She was the dream candidate -- experienced, proactive, knowledgeable, professional. You would be an IDIOT not to hire her. She got called back for a second interview and we went into high-witch spellcraft gear.

The day before the interview she went to yoga and took a long bath. She created an altar in her living room and spoke her prayers to the moon. She wrote affirmations on a scroll of paper and stuck it into a tiny bottle filled with glitter, then sealed the bottle with wax from her altar.

The next day she dressed herself to perfection and nestled her secret spell bottle between her breasts. She aced the interview and the whole company fell in love with her. They told her they would be in touch very soon. She wrote them a heartfelt thank you letter, and then...

Nothing.

Nada.

Zilch.

No word from them ever again.

Vivi was crestfallen. Heartbroken. She had all her eggs in this basket. She thought she had this. Now she was back to shaking the trees on Craigslist.

We all know this feeling. The feeling when you are so certain that something is going to happen, or something is meant for you, or someone is your soulmate. We all simultaneously know the frustration of having that ripped from our arms like a metaphorical unborn baby. Our precious creation, our plan for how things are supposed to go, gone in an instant.

These experiences can be grandiose (like being in a relationship with someone you have fallen in love with for months and all of a sudden they drop off the face of the earth and you never hear from them again) or trivial (you walk to the subway at normal pace on your way to an appointment, and all of a sudden the doors close way too fast and you are left standing on the platform like a schmuck.)

WTF universe????

These moments are when the motto of all great seductresses saves my ass every single time: Rejection is protection. Close your eyes and think of something in your life that you really love and value. A person, a place, a thing. See it really clearly.

Now, reflect on the journey you took to establish that presence in your life. How many things had to go wrong for that to go right?

"Thank God for unanswered prayers."
— *Garth Brooks song*

This is a key component of what makes seduction such a spiritual practice. In the traditional paradigm of seduction, we operate under the belief that if life is flowing and we are getting what we want things are good, and we are good at seduction. If we are not in the flow and life is a shit storm we are bad at it. But remember, in sacred seduction there is no good or bad, no real right or wrong. All of it is just threads in the tapestry that makes up The Seductive Life.

"Hearts break so they can open."

— *Rochelle Schieck*

When I am really excited about something, say, a date with a fetching suitor, I allow myself to feel the fullness of my excitement in one hand. Simultaneously, in my other hand I hold the very real possibility that anything could happen — I could get stood up, this person could cancel at the last minute, I could get lost on my way to the date and never find the place. Why? When I allow myself to stay soft, open and fluid to any outcome, I leave room for an even better experience to occur than the one my human plans could ever provide.

In choosing to be open to any outcome rather than controlling of it, a good time is always guaranteed.

I know this comes right up against the practice of positive thinking. Don't get me wrong, I am not a pessimist. The philosophy that our thoughts become our reality is spot on and can make magic happen. I believe this wholeheartedly and I practice it regularly. But this mindset can become tricky, and fool us into thinking that if things go our way we are a good little manifester and if they don't, we messed up.

Leaving ourselves open to the idea that rejection is actually just a form of protection takes the right or wrong out of the equation, leaving us with the simple truth of what life really is: delightfully unpredictable. I am willing to both follow and lead in the dance.

To bring our story full circle, where is Vivi now? The rejection of the job she thought she wanted made room for the job she actually wanted, which is the job she has now. One thing to know about Vivi, even though she works in corporate America, she is a rare bird and a flamboyant creature if ever there was one. The job she has now is in the same field and is the same type of position, but in this office her colleagues welcome and embrace her individuality, rather than ask her to stuff it down. This is an immeasurable gift to my creative fire storm of a friend. She recently instituted "bow-tie Mondays and bombshell Fridays". Every Monday all the men have to wear bow ties and every Friday the ladies have to wear red lipstick. No exceptions.

Thanks to the rejection she experienced from the previous interview, rather than being a black sheep, she is loved for being exactly who God/Goddess created her to be: a gorgeous, bright, vibrant pink flamingo.

GETTING WHAT IT IS YOU REALLY WANT

*"We get what we want,
not what we ask for."*

— *Unknown*

In an earlier chapter we talked about the two building blocks of seductive success:

action + attraction = seduction

The way we navigate our seduction efforts in the direction we desire is with this final point to the triangle: INTENTION.

Our intentions shape everything we do, have and experience. The intention is what can make a sales pitch seem straightforward or slimy. It can make a sarcastic joke come out hurtful or hilarious. The words can be exactly the same, but depending on the intention, the outcome completely different.

Let's say you are preparing for a date with a new person. You want to look hot, so you decide to wear your new sexy boots that come up to the knee and have an insanely high heel. Your feet are already tired from running around all day and even though your flat booties are really what calls to you in that moment, beauty is pain right? So let's do this.

You meet up with your date at a bar. Live music is playing and the place is packed. There is not a seat in sight. Fifteen minutes pass and your toes are on fire, your lower back feels like two pieces of a puzzle that don't remotely fit together. You are cranky and can't hear your date. You have a sullen look on your face. You resent your date for not noticing your sexy boots. Finally you assert your need for a seat and end up in a far corner of the bar that smells like hot dogs. You fear that you seem high maintenance, so you feel uncomfortable and quiet.

The kicker is that from your date's perspective, he or she is one of those rare birds that finds high heels unattractive. He or she doesn't understand why a person would wobble along on stilts all day, and yearns for something that simply frames the foot and leg, not blocks the whole darn picture.

You, of course, have no way of knowing this fact, so you take your date's lack of response to mean rejection and leave the bar pissed off at your date, yourself, and while we're at it, God.

WOOF.

Does this sound familiar? For your sake, I hope not. But to me, it is one example of many experiences where I placed more attention on my ego than my true intention and therefore, the night was a bust.

In the scenario illustrated above, the intention is along the lines of:

- Make this person think I am sexy

- Have them like me

- Look hot and therefore, guarantee a good night

If we were to take a moment to feel more deeply into the true intention for the evening, it may look something more like this:

- To enjoy myself, enjoy this new person, and learn as much as I can about him or her

- To feel sexy on all fronts, body, mind and soul

- To laugh my ass off

- To have a moment of intense eye contact that is loaded with tension and precedes a kiss

The first set of intentions may seem shallow, but if we look closely the goal is actually the same — to have an enjoyable evening. The main difference? The first set of intentions is about maintaining control. The second is about surrendering it.

Be it a lover or a parking spot, setting your intention of what you wish to seduce and then surrendering the outcome is the way to guaranteed seductive success.

When we pull back our arrow, take the best aim we can muster, and leave the results up to those forces that are greater than us we initiate the most beautiful dance between our desire and our divinity. Our arrow may not hit the bulls eye; it might miss by a mile. But that is the thing about seductive surrender.

When we follow where our desires lead us, even if it is in the opposite direction to where we think we should be going, we will always end up where we really want to be in the end.

STORIES FROM THE
SEDUCTION COUNCIL

WHAT DOES IT MEAN TO YOU TO BE A SACRED SEDUCTRESS?

"As a person who actively practices her religion, since taking classes with Kitty I have seen the parallels in the practice of my faith to the practices that Kitty encourages in her teaching. The rituals, the lighting of candles, the celebration of milestones, the sacredness that Kitty's practices bring to one's life offer something that feels very familiar to me, but this time the context is one's own femininity, selfhood, and well-being."

— *Eliza*

"SURRENDER. Awed. Grateful. Laughing. Firmly nestled in the experience of sadness while it's going on and not trying to escape. Embracing of all facets of experience."

— *Nikki*

"It's living the life that I was born to live. I spent decades trying to fit in a box of "good girl" "fat girl who hated her body," "People pleaser," "professional care taker," and guess what none of it fit. It got to the point that it was a life or death action. Finding sacred seduction helped me get back home. I was able to own my intuitive, most loving self. It triggered me to do massive edits in my life, removing all of the toxic behaviors and relationships that no longer belong."

— *Laura*

"In my body, flowing, unfolding, allowing, moving through life with more confidence, self love, self acceptance, from the bottoms of my feet to the very top of my head. To me, being the Sacred Seductress means I LOVE all of me."

— *Sofia*

"Being a sacred seductress means going with the flow of life, rather than trying to push my will on it. I am all for conjuring and manifesting. But sometimes it is all so exhausting. Being a sacred seductress means that I can sit back and surrender to the goodies the Universe has in store. I can decide I want to walk down a different street than usual and discover flowering trees, cute puppies, a farmers market I never knew was there, and perhaps bump into an old friend. These things come easily to a seductress, because she is open to the surprises life can bring. Life seduces her, and she seduces life. It's incredibly fun!"

— *Sandi*

CHAPTER 8

SEDUCTION
IS A WAY OF LIFE

What does it mean to live seduction?

- We trust in the tides of desire.

- We are unafraid to attract attention, and we invite opportunities to bless the world with our radiance.

- We flirt with everything.

- We go through life sensually, feeling our way.

- We love ourselves for who we are, not who we think we should be.

- We can make ritual out of the simplest of things.

- Our "flaws" are our greatest assets.

- Our vulnerability is one of the sexiest thing about us.

- We find the divine in beauty.

- We are willing to say no to the things we don't want in service to the things we do.

- We know that our flesh is the holiest of holies.

- We believe that shame is not a reason to back down; it is just an invitation to own ourselves more fully.

- We trust our anger and use it as a sword to carve away that which no longer serves us or the world.

- Our sensuality is our superpower.

- We dress, speak, love and live with sparkle, sass and flair.

- We do not try to fit in; we make the world fit around us.

- We live life as one long love affair.

One of the things that makes a sacred seductress so unique is her willingness to listen to the stirrings of her soul on the inside and allow her life to be an expression of that on the outside.

*Every seductress is different in
her unique code of captivation.*

If I asked you to imagine yourself as the ideal seductress, what would life look like to you? Would you wake up on a life size powder puff to the caress of your lovers hands over your silken skin? Or would you rise from a big cotton bed and step onto your balcony to kiss the Mediterranean Sea good morning? Would you wake to the smell of burning sage wafting in from the ceremonial morning gratitude offering in your shamanic village? Or perhaps you awake to the feeling of hard steel under your soft body, looking out on a tiny county jail cell after a night of raising hell?

Answer these questions as if you are a fly on the wall of your ultimate seduction fantasy. If you lived the sacred seduction lifestyle full out.

Don't think about it too much. This is a game you can play over and over again, as our seductive nature is never static. It is always flowing, growing and shape shifting.

WHO IS YOUR SACRED SEDUCTRESS?

- The first thing she does when she wakes up in the morning is:

- Three words that would describe her best are:

- Her best friend would say she is:

- Her lovers would say she is:

- Her inspiration is/are:

- The thing she fights most fiercely for on the planet is:

- She would never:

- **In her closet you will find:**

- **Her home is decorated with lots of:**

- **When she walks down the street:**

- **The thing she is most known for is:**

Now, take that information and write "A day in the life". How does your seductress spend her morning? Her afternoon? Her evening? Her midnight hour?

Extra credit: Share your seduction fantasy aloud with your Seduction Society and ask your fellow seductresses to fill in any details you may have missed.

I PUT A SPELL ON YOU
Seductive Ritual, Magic and Enchantment

When I was a kid, I did not grow up thinking I would become a seduction teacher. Actually, I wanted to become a nun when I grew up. I loved religion and going to church. What I especially loved was the ritual of it. On Sunday mornings, before everyone else woke up, I would rearrange our kitchen into Sunday Mass. I would lay out the white tablecloth, put on my Dad's bathrobe and my Mom's scarf, line up the benches and chairs for my participants, cut the Wonder Bread into circles, and pour grape juice into the wine glass. When everyone would come downstairs, groggy and cranky, I would beg them to sit in on my service. I would deliver communion, perform baptisms, and even give the occasional exalted sermon, as pictured here.

Fast forward to age 16 when I couldn't be more disinterested in organized religion. That was the year of *The Craft*, a film about four teenage girls who discover they have magical powers and use them to wreak havoc on their all-girls prep school, eventually ending up destroying one another. Think *Mean Girls* with black magic.

I wasn't interested in black magic at all, but the idea of wielding magic with our intentions and our hands drove me straight to the bookstore to find everything related to witchcraft and spell casting (and drove my mother nuts with worry that I was headed for a career in occult satanism).

I came across *The Supermarket Sorceress* by Lexa Roséan. It was filled with all sorts of homemade recipes for casting a spell and creating a result. For my budding teenage brain, however, I wanted fast, guaranteed results. I remember sprinkling fennel seeds on the telephone to make my crush call me. It didn't work.

In the wonderful book *Romancing the Ordinary* by Sarah Ban Breathnach, the author quotes her friend, teacher and fellow author, Barrie Dolnick: "The practice of casting spells is an unconscious ritual in our society. For instance, when you put on perfumes you are amplifying your own energy through scent, which can make you more attractive to others. A gift of red roses is a common spell, eliciting passionate energy between you and your loved one."

Breathnach continues: "If you have an important meeting, do you wear a special outfit or a favorite piece of jewelry or even try to schedule the meeting for a specific time of day? You're unconsciously casting a success spell.

When you arrange a bouquet of flowers for your home's foyer, simmer cinnamon on the stove in the winter, set out bowls of intoxicating rose potpourri in the summer, or light candles at the dinner table, you are unconsciously casting spells (called atmospheres) to make your home more inviting. Do you listen to a certain CD to put you in the mood as you're doing your makeup before you go out in the evening? As Etta James's, Tori Amos's or Aretha's vibrations steadily raise your psychic energy, you're subtly but powerfully casting an ancient sexual enchantment.

A spell is an organized desire passionately, creatively, and personally sent out into the Universe through words and ritual — a three dimensional prayer that engages all your senses".

The piece I was missing with the fennel seeds is what Breathnach mentions above. It is not about the objects, it is about the intention.

I can cast a spell by doing something as simple as putting on my mascara. I pay close attention to how the black goo magnifies the windows to my soul. I feel how the practice of exaggerating my eyes connects me to my ancestresses. With each stroke I utter a silent prayer of that which I wish to open my eyes to, and that which I wish to be revealed.

It is really so simple to be a witch.

There are many books and resources out there about herbs, oils, times of day, chants to incant and many other details to enhance your ritual. I think that inventing your own rituals is most powerful though, as it ties us on a deeply personal level to that which we are creating.

I once had a student who created a mandala out of empty cupcake wrappers that she filled with different items that she used to symbolize her intentions for the ritual. Everything from rose petals for love, cotton buds to give gratitude for the softness of life, even piece of deer poop from the woods to symbolize letting go! The possibilities are truly endless.

BATHING RITUAL

Items you will need:

- 3 things you can add to enhance your bath. Examples would be: Epsom salts, flower petals, essential oils, bubble bath/body wash, a water-safe object that has meaning to you like a pebble or a shell

- A few candles

- A book or magazine that relaxes you (erotica is really good to read in the bath!)

- Your favorite music

- A towel and lotion for after the bath

1. Prepare

Begin by cleaning the tub, making it fit for a Queen. As you scrub, do so with the intention of buffing away anything that doesn't serve you in your body and life. You don't have to think about these things as you scrub, just holding the intention will do the trick.

When the tub is clean, fill it with as much water as it will hold! While the tub is filling, grab a clean towel and fold it nicely. Press play on your music.

2. Create Sacred Space

Light the candles. As you light each candle envision each of them representing angels of sensuality that are there to protect you and hold a sacred space for you to complete your ritual.

3. Dress Your Bath

Take a moment with each item you have chosen to add to the water. Infuse each item with your intention. You can turn any ordinary object into a powerful piece of magic just with your thoughts and intentions. For example, when I sprinkle Epsom salts into my bath, I first hold the salts and say, "These salts will draw everything from my body that keeps me from love. These salts are of the Earth, I am of the Earth. These salts make this water feel like a hug from the Earth itself."

I then add pure essential oils. As I add lavender, I say, "This oil will bring soothing energy to my bath, easing any stress or tension in my feminine soul." As I add the rose oil: "This oil will infuse me with all the beauty, radiance and perfection of a summer rose in full bloom." As I add the jasmine oil: "This oil infuses me with the exoticism of the Goddess, her mystery, her intrigue, and her irresistibility."

Whatever items you choose, they are perfect. You can even use table sugar to add more sweetness to your life. It is your intention that gives them their power. Get creative and don't hold back!

4. Step In

Step in slowly and savor every moment of sitting back into the water, letting it swirl around you. Feel as much as you can. Caress your skin under the water. Let the music soothe you. Close your eyes and breathe in the steam, the scents, the moment.

If it feels right, pick up your book or magazine. If you like meditation, do that instead. Maybe journaling is your jam. Choose whatever puts a stop to the racing thought patterns in your mind and allows your body to fully relax.

Float in the bath for as long as you like, a minimum of 20 minutes. Get out when it feels right. Not when you need to baste the chicken, not when you are bored and want to check your e-mail. When it feels right to your body, then you may step out of the bath.

5. Step Out

When you feel complete, close your eyes and envision Aphrodite, a Goddess born of the sea. As you stand up, feel yourself as a Goddess: renewed, regenerated and reborn, a different woman now than the woman that stepped into that water.

Envelop yourself in your freshly folded towel. While your skin is still slightly damp, slather yourself with twice the lotion/cream you would normally use. Get your whole body nice and slick. Then, let your hands run wild all over your skin. Massage, caress and bless yourself with your own hands until the cream starts to absorb. Play with vigorous touch and slow touch. Make sure not to leave a single inch of your body unloved.

When you are finished in the space, thank the Earth, thank the water, thank yourself for taking this time, and thank the Goddess for making you exactly who you are on this day.

"We gain strength, and courage, and confidence by each experience in which we really stop to look fear in the face...we must do that which we think we cannot."

— *Eleanor Roosevelt*

A SEDUCTRESS DOES NOT ACT ALONE

As I hope you have seen through the sharing of the exercises in this book with your Seduction Society, a seductress does not act alone. Seduction takes a village. Remember, the seductress is the ultimate feminist. She seeks community over competition. She works to empower others rather than sabotage their vehicles in the race to the finish. She is not in a race. She is taking her own sweet time, because she does not care if she wins or loses. Because she is confident in her seductive power, she has already won it all.

"I am in competition with no one.
I hope we all make it."
— *Unknown*

Bridging the gap between women is one of the most fundamental things we can do to make this world a more kind, friendly, peaceful place.

There is a common misconception that a seductress is an isolated creature. When we think of a seductress we often see a red-lipped, raven-haired vamp sipping a martini alone at a hotel bar. Or perhaps she is the one holding court at a dinner party, surrounded by a crowd of male admirers while snide glances float across the room from her female competitors. A seductress is not someone we picture in the company of other women. It is this exact birdcage of separateness that has kept the seductress's innate and sacred power in a state of imprisonment. Seduction does not happen in isolation. It happens in community, family and partnership.

Creating community and thawing the deep freeze of competition between women is one of the most positive things we can do for this world. A woman who loves and supports other women is extremely seductive and attractive. Expanding your sacred seduction community offers endless rewards for you, and for all of humankind.

CREATING COMMUNITY

- Compliment other women with complete abandon.

- Make it the new normal for women to praise each other's beauty.

- Be gratuitous with praise.

- Feel your praise down to your very bones and don't be shy, fortune favors the bold!

- Flash her those pearly whites! Sometimes just a simple smile or hello can dispel thousands of years of cultural isolation.

- See the beauty in every woman. Every woman on Earth possesses an enchanting, intoxicating beauty. All we need to do is look more closely than we have been taught. We see her beauty, she sees her beauty. A woman who knows the eternal nature of her beauty is a woman who recognizes her divinity, and gets a peek at yours as well. Win, win, win, win, win.

- Make it safe to be successful. Women can be hasty with the celebration of their accomplishments. If you catch even a whiff of good news, sprinkle pixie dust on it for her and make it safe for her successes and good fortune to go forward and multiply. It all starts with us.

As the saying goes, be the change you wish to see. Model sacred seduction, enjoy the fuck out of yourself and your life, and others will not be able to help themselves from hitching onto your wagon and following suit.

SEDUCTION COUNCIL

DESCRIBE A DAY IN THE LIFE OF YOUR SACRED SEDUCTRESS

"A breeze blowing through her window, gauzy curtains blowing and softly grazing her feet. The sound of harp music gently awakening her from her sleep. She awakens to beauty. Paintings of Venus. Sculptures. A white airy majestic creamy boudoir. A lovely array of things to decorate her body with. A place to meditate by the ocean."

— *Alia*

"She wakes up and lights candles, meditate, center for the day. She goes outside first thing, to stretch and move and enjoy the flavor of the light and the air that day, soaking up nature. She peppers her day with small delights. Lots of art and music. Delicious coffee. Pleasure and physical affection...."

— *Nikki*

"Fresh breezes drift in through the open window, and the sound of the sea in the distance slowly awakens her. A tray of luscious fresh fruits awaits, and the promise of a walk in the soft sand when she is ready, camera around her neck, to capture the natural beauty all around her. Her children play happily in the waves, supervised by her beloved husband, whose idea it was for her to sleep in while he took the children down to the beach. She spends the morning wandering the dunes, photographing everything that catches her eye, filling her camera with beautiful shots that she will enjoy editing later on. Then she joins her family for a picnic lunch on the beach, watching the children laugh and play until it is time for a bike ride along the shoreline, followed by a twilight dinner, bedtime for the children, and then a romantic, moonlit time with her beloved, making love under the stars on a blanket in the sand, just out of earshot of the beach house."

— *Eliza*

"A sacred seductress wakes up whenever is comfortable for her to do so, she sleeps in a soft comfortable bed surrounded by beauty. She eats healthfully but delicious foods, she takes long walks, she dresses beautifully everyday for her own pleasure. She tends to her mind body and spirit and surrounds herself with people on a spiritual path. She does not waste her time with people who are not interested in a meaningful life."

— *Beelzebabe*

"This seductress loves to start the day with yoga inspired movement to her seductive playlist followed by sitting in silence and breathing deeply into her hips and dedicating her day to the Divine Feminine within her. To begin this ritual candles are lit on an altar dedicated to the Divine Feminine and it is very sacred. After the candles are blown out the day is off and running and the altar serves as a reminder throughout the day of my feminine power and sensuality. If needed a spontaneous, scintillatingly sensual dance break may erupt to diffuse erratic energy. My morning is my sacred time to remember my seductress and invoke her energy into my day."

— *Coco Divine*

WHAT WORDS OF ADVICE DO YOU HAVE FOR A BUDDING SACRED SEDUCTRESS?

"Start with soft sweet bites. You are a budding rose. Majestic!"

— *Alia*

"Don't worry — trust your own goodness, the goodness of your desires."

— *Nikki*

"It's a practice that builds on itself and it gets more seductive the more you practice! It's all about SEDUCING yourself, not about seducing anyone else."

— *Sofia*

"As I apply seduction to my life, Kitty's voice often pops into my head "What is seducing you right now?" That often guides me to my next right action. Any and every aspect of your life can be seductive. It's a beautiful dance between you and the divine. Illness, divorce, family, children, romance, friendships, work, shopping, taking a walk, doing the dishes, ordering a coffee... all of it is an opportunity to allow yourself to be seduced, do some seducing, and see what magic can unfold. And there will be magic!"

— *Sandi*

"Trust yourself to be the Queen that you are inside. Don't be afraid to step outside the bounds of what — and who — people know you to be. Know that many women have gone before you on this path, blazing a beautiful trail for you to either follow or create your own. And don't forget that lipstick and a little bit of sexy lingerie can really rev up your day, and that of all those around you!!"

— Eliza

"No matter how un-seductive you feel right now, it's a self-illusion. Your light is within you if you can look in the face of your own unique beauty."

— Beelzebabe

"When in doubt...wink!"

— Coco

"From the moment I was six I felt sexy. And let me tell you it was hell, sheer hell, waiting to do something about it."

— Bette Davis

CLOSURE

DANCE ME TO THE END

How does one bring closure to a story of seduction?

The truth is one cannot.

In the realm of sacred seduction, there is no end, just as there is no beginning. Our seductive power never ceases, just as it has been there all along. Rather than being a maze where the object is to figure out the path and reach the end, sacred seduction is a labyrinth. A winding path where the only way out is the way you came in. The intention is the journey, not the destination.

To quote Esther Perel on foreplay, "foreplay begins at the end of the previous orgasm." So it is with seduction. We are always seducing and being seduced. We do not seek the end because in doing so we would miss the adventure. Seduction, like love, is infinite.

So with that secret sense of knowing that is so essential to our craft, I invite you to enjoy these lyrics to one of seduction's anthems, Dance Me To The End Of Love, by the musical mystic, Leonard Cohen.

Dance me to your beauty with a burning violin
Dance me through the panic 'til I'm gathered safely in
Lift me like an olive branch and be my homeward dove
Dance me to the end of love
Dance me to the end of love
Oh let me see your beauty when the witnesses are gone
Let me feel you moving like they do in Babylon
Show me slowly what I only know the limits of
Dance me to the end of love
Dance me to the end of love

Dance me to the wedding now, dance me on and on
Dance me very tenderly and dance me very long

We're both of us beneath our love, we're both of us above
Dance me to the end of love
Dance me to the end of love

Dance me to the children who are asking to be born
Dance me through the curtains that our kisses have outworn
Raise a tent of shelter now, though every thread is torn
Dance me to the end of love

Dance me to your beauty with a burning violin
Dance me through the panic till I'm gathered safely in
Touch me with your naked hand or touch me with your glove
Dance me to the end of love
Dance me to the end of love
Dance me to the end of love

The yin and the yang of seduction, the beginning and the end, the longing and satisfaction.

The feminine and the masculine, the being and the doing, the wanting and the having.

The light and the dark, the stroke and the slap, the temptation and the first forbidden bite…

On your journey of all these things, I wish you well.

PHOTO CREDITS

p. 10, 44, 74, 101, 137 — Beth Mayesh

p. 12 — Pixabay

p. 24 — Becca Kannapel

p. 28 — Alberto Vargas

Cover, p. 33, 72, 135 — Burke Heffner

p. 73, 103, 108, 167 — Sharon Birke, Powerful Goddess Photography

p. 49 — Déjeuner sur l'herbe by Monet

p. 50 — Rose Petals: Creative Commons "Simply Beautiful" by Audrey

p. 51 — Figs by Clemens v. Vogelsang

p. 52 — Asparagus by Liz West

p. 71 — Maya Angelou by Academy of Achievement

p. 113 — Cleopatra by J.W. Waterhouse

p. 157 — Eleanor Roosevelt, National Archives and Records Administration

*All other images are part of the public domain.

ABOUT THE AUTHOR

Kitty Cavalier is a full-time seductress. She believes seduction can't be taught — it can only be experienced. She travels the globe offering seduction workshops, retreats and experiences for women, ranging from one-on-one mentoring to in-the-flesh gatherings and her open diary. Her work has been featured on The Daily Love, The Good Men Project, Psychology Today, Penthouse, Elle.com Horoscopes, Glimpse TV with Kate Northrup, and more. Sacred Seduction is her first book. She lives in Brooklyn, NY.

To contact Kitty or learn more, visit www.kittycavalier.com.